German Cuisine

- Easy to Imitate -

THE BEST 51 GERMAN DISHES

German Recipes and how to cook them Successfully

**The most important German recipes.
Simple and more difficult recipes made easy!**

German food is something for food lovers

and not really suitable for a diet.

Usually, pictures are great imaginative expectations of what to cook.

German dishes don't always look so nice, and in German cuisine, it's not all about looks. Many professional and hobby chefs just want to get some tasty food and new inspiration. I know that some if they look at this cookbook, might be disappointed by the missing pictures. But I would rather offer more recipes than various pictures of what it might look like, but we both know this is not how it will look in the end. So the only pictures in this book are on the cover :)

Learn how to cook in Germany. Just cook German recipes, main courses, sauces or side dishes and bring a piece of Germany into your home

What are the most important ingredients in a German kitchen? Potatoes, beer, pork, cabbage and butter!

For more german recipes search for "The German Kitchen"

For life inspiration through short stories search for "Akira White"

Now let us begin!

All Recipes

Grießbrei
Semolina pudding

Königsberger Klopse
Koenigsberg meatballs

Salzbraten
Salt Roast

Spaetzle

Käsespätzle
Cheese spaetzle

Schweinebraten mit dunkler Brotsoße
Roast pork with dark bread sauce

Norddeutsche Erbsensuppe
North German pea soup

Erbsensuppe klassisch
Pea soup classic

Erbseneintopf
Pea stew

Rehbraten
Roast venison

Berliner Kartoffelsalat
Berlin potato salad

Klassischer Kartoffelsalat
Classic potato salad

Norddeutscher Kartoffelsalat
North German potato salad

Hühner Frikassee
Chicken fricassee

Spargel mit Schweinefilet und Pilzsoße
Asparagus with pork tenderloin and mushroom sauce

Frikadellen
rissoles

Rösti
hash browns

Käse-Lauchsuppe
Cheese and leek soup

Gulasch
Goulash

Grüne Bohnensuppe
Green bean soup

Senf-Eier
Mustard eggs

Labskaus
lobscouse

Zwiebelkuchen
Onion cake

Blumenkohl & Brokkoli Auflauf
Cauliflower and Broccoli Casserole

Grünkohl
green cabbage

Grünkohl

Grützwurst mit Kartoffelpüree
Grützwurst with mashed potatoes

Jägerschnitzel
Hunter's Schnitzel

Kartoffelsuppe
Potato soup

Hackbällchen mit Kartoffelspalten
Meatballs with potato wedges

Leber
Liver

Gans
Goose

Gänsebraten
Roast goose

Krautsalat
Coleslaw

Wirsing-Eintopf mit Kasseler
Savoy-cabbage-stew with cured pork

Muscheln
Mussels

Maultaschen
Swabian raviolis

Sauerbraten
marinated pot roast

Ente
Duck

Hochzeitssuppe
Wedding Soup

Kohlrouladen
Cabbage rolls

Eingelegte Bratheringe
Pickled fried herrings

Schupfnudeln
potato noodles

Berliner Kartoffelsuppe
Berliner potato soup

Rinderrouladen
Beef roulades

Krustenbraten
Roast crust

Schweinshaxen
Knuckles of pork

Pilz-Sahnesoße
Mushroom cream sauce

Linsen mit Würstchen
Lentils with sausages

Brezeln
Pretzels

Semmelknödel
Dumplings

For me, the following recipes are the most important recipes that have accompanied me through my culinary life in Germany.

There are countless recipes, but here are the best ones.

Grießbrei
Semolina pudding

Working time 10 to 20 minutes

Total time 20 to 30 minutes

For 4 portions

Ingredients

850 ml milk (in the best case 3,5 % fat)
85 g wheat semolina
40 g sugar
8 g vanilla sugar
0,1 g salt
1 egg
30 g butter

Preparation

Step 1

Put milk, sugar, vanilla sugar and salt in a pot.

Step 2
Bring the pot to boil.

Step 3
Add the wheat semolina and mix with a whisk.

Step 4
Set the pot aside.
Let it cool down for 7 minutes.

Step 5
Separate the egg yolk from the egg white.

Step 6
Beat the egg whites with a whisk until stiff.

Step 7
Add the egg yolks and butter to the warm semolina porridge.

Step 8:
Stir the semolina until the butter has melted.

Step 9:
Stir the egg white into the finished semolina porridge.

It is often eaten with cinnamon and sugar or apple sauce.
Instead of sugar, you can also simply use sweetener

It can be garnished according to your heart's desire.

Königsberger Klopse
Koenigsberg meatballs

Working time approx. 45 minutes

Total time approx. 1 hour 25 minutes

For 4 portions

Ingredients

Required ingredients for the meatballs

300 g minced beef
200 g minced pork
1 soft roll
1 large onion
2 eggs
30 g breadcrumbs
salt and pepper
10g anchovy paste

Required ingredients for the broth

1-litre clear meat broth
Salt
2 medium-sized onions
1 bay leaf
3 grains allspice

3 peppercorns

For the sauce

45g butter
30 g flour
Sugar
lemon juice 375 ml
Broth of meat 125 ml
Cream 200ml
Capers
1 egg yolk
salt and pepper

Preparation

preparation of the meatballs

Step 1
Cut onions into fine cubes. Finely chop the bread rolls.

Step 2
Put the minced meat, bread roll and onion in a bowl with two eggs, salt and pepper and knead a smooth meat dough.

Step 3
Bind the dumpling dough with breadcrumbs and anchovy paste.

Step 4
Form the dough into lumps.

preparation of the broth

Step 1
Add onions and spices to the broth.

Step 2
Heat broth.

Step 3
Add the meatballs to the stock for 10 minutes and simmer.

Step 4
Remove the bay leaf, peppercorns and pimento from the stock.
Wait 10 minutes.

Step 5
Remove the dumplings and keep warm.

preparation of the sauce

Step 1
Heat the butter.
Add flour. Add stock.
Add capers and cream a little later.

Step 2
Reduce temperature.
Add lemon juice, sugar, salt and pepper.

Step 3
Stir the egg yolks into the sauce and add the beaters.

Salzbraten
Salt Roast

Working time approx. 5 minutes

Total time approx. 2.5 hours

Ingredients

Roast pork approx. 2 kg
500 g salt
Pepper

Preparation

Step 1
Preheat the oven to 220 °C top/bottom heat (also with circulating air).

Step 2
Fleisch mit Pfeffer würzen.

Step 3
Put salt on a baking tray and place the meat on top.

Step 4
Leave for about 2.5 hours in the open without opening.

Potato salad can be served with it.

Spaetzle

Working time: 30 minutes

Total time approx. 45 minutes

For 4 portions

Ingredients

550 g flour
6 eggs
250 ml milk
30 g butter, melted
Salt

Preparation

Step 1
Melt the butter and let it cool down.

Step 2
Put flour, eggs, milk, salt and the butter in a large bowl.

Step 3
Mix everything to a tough, sticky dough.

Step 4

Let the dough rise for 5 - 10 minutes.

Step 5

In a large pot, bring water to the boil and salt.

Step 6

Spread the dough on a board and scrape the spaetzle off the board (or use a spaetzle tool).

Step 7

Elongated drops are formed.

Step 8

Let it boil until the spaetzle floats on the water and then skim it.

Käsespätzle
Cheese spaetzle

Working time approx. 50 minutes

Total time approx. 55 minutes

For 4 portions

Ingredients

500 g flour
5 eggs
125 ml litre mineral water
Salt
250 g cheese (Emmental)
3 large onions
Butter
Saltwater

---

preparation

Step 1
Peel and thinly slice the onions.

Step 2
Fry the onions in butter.

Step 3
Mix flour with eggs, water and salt.

Step 4
Stir the dough vigorously until bubbles form.
Then set aside.

Step 5
Bring a pot with water and salt to 90 °C.
Grate the cheese.

Step 6
Place the dough on a board and scrape into thin strips in the water.
Boil until they float.
Then skim them.

Step 7
Place the spaetzle in a casserole dish alternating layers of cheese. Place at 100 °C for about 15 minutes.

Step 8
Spread the onions from step 1 on top.

Salad is a good accompaniment.

Schweinebraten mit dunkler Brotsoße
Roast pork with dark bread sauce

Working time approx. 45 minutes

Total time approx. 45 minutes

Ingredients

About 2 kg roast pork
(Carve the rind several times before)
3 medium-sized onions
2 carrots
750 ml vegetable broth
500 ml dark beer
1 stick of leek
4 end slices sourdough bread
salt and pepper
Paprika powder
Coriander
5 cloves of garlic
ground caraway seeds

Preparation

Step 1
Rub the meat with a mixture of salt, pepper, coriander,

garlic and ground caraway.

Step 2
Preheat the oven to 220 °C.

Step 3
Cut onions, carrots and leek and bread into small cubes.

Step 4
In a large tall pan or roasting pan, sear the meat from all six sides without the spices burning.

Step 5
Once all sides have been fried for at least a minute, add the vegetables.

Step 6
Continue frying until the vegetables are lightly browned.

Step 7
Finally, add caraway and garlic and line with the bread.

Step 8
Place the pan or roaster with lid in the oven at reduced 200 °C (top and bottom heat) for about 40 minutes.

Step 9
Then reduce the temperature in the oven to 180 °C. And boil the broth.

Step 10
Mix the beer with the broth and then pour into the pan/roaster until the bread is covered.

Step 11
Wait three hours.
Then remove from the oven and let it cool slightly in the air.

Step 12
Puree the contents of the pan to a mass.

It is recommended to serve boiled potatoes with the dish.

Norddeutsche Erbsensuppe
North German pea soup

Working time approx. 20 minutes

Total time approx. 1 hour 20 minutes

For 4 portions

Ingredients

250 g green peas
1 large onion
1 clove of garlic
1-litre vegetable stock
200 g sour cream
4 g dill, chopped
150 g prawns
100 g smoked salmon
salt and pepper
4 g lemon juice
Butter

Preparation

Step 1
Cut onion and garlic into small cubes and fry in butter.
Add the peas.
Add vegetable stock. Bring to the boil, then reduce the temperature.
Wait one hour and stir in between.

Step 2
Add salt, pepper, dill and sour cream.
Puree everything.

Step 3
Cut the salmon into small pieces, arrange on plates with the crabs and pour over the soup, serve hot immediately.

With a few slices of toast.

Erbsensuppe klassisch
Pea soup classic

Working time approx. 30 minutes

Total time approx. 14 hours 30 minutes

For 4 portions

Ingredients

150 g peas
500 ml of water
150 g belly bacon
100 g leek
100 g carrot
50 g celery (peeled)
150 g potato
1 bay leaf
1 onion
20 g butter
250 ml meat broth

Pepper
250 g Mettwurst[1]

Preparation

Step 1
Soak the peas in 500 ml water overnight.

Step 2
Chop onion, potatoes, carrot and leek into rings.

Step 3
Bring peas and water to the boil.

Step 4
After about 30 minutes, add the pancetta and cook for 30 minutes.

Step 5
Add leek, carrots, potatoes and bay leaf.

Step 6
Fry the onion in a pan with oil. Then add to the soup. Add the celery and broth. Cook again for 30 minutes.

Step 7
Remove celery, bay leaf and pancetta.

Step 8
Mash the soup a little with a masher.

Step 9

Cut bacon into small pieces and add to the soup with the sausage and pepper.

Step 10

Finally, cook for 30 minutes and stir.

Erbseneintopf
Pea stew

Working time approx. 25 minutes

Total time approx. 1 hour 35 minutes

For 4 portions

Ingredients

500 g peas
100 g celeriac
100 g carrots
150 g leek
2 large onions
350 g potatoes
150 g belly bacon
35 g butter
7 g marjoram
2 litres of water
40 g vegetable broth (powder)
Salt
white pepper

Preparation

Step 1
Cut bacon, onions, carrots, celery, leek and potatoes into small cubes.

Step 2
Melt the butter in a saucepan at low heat.

Step 3
Fry bacon, onions, then add carrots, celery and leek.

Step 4
Add the peas and two litres of water.

Step 5
Bring everything to the boil, then add the broth and marjoram.

Step 6
Simmer for about 20 minutes and then add the potatoes, salt and pepper.

Step 7
Simmer for 40 minutes and stir several times.

Rehbraten

Roast venison

Working time approx. 1 hour

Total time approx. 2 days 1 hour

Ingredients

2000 g of venison
1,5 litre buttermilk
300 ml red wine (semi-dry)
35 g spice mixture[2]
30 g butter
2 cups of sour cream
1.5 litres of broth
300 ml red wine (dry)
1 carrot
1 garlic bulb
5 juniper berries
4 onions
200 g wild mushrooms
Jam (e.g. apple or wild berries)
salt and pepper

Preparation

Step 1
Chop onions, garlic and carrots.

Step 2
The meat is soaked for 48 hours in a mixture of 300 ml red wine, 1500 ml buttermilk, garlic and the spice mixture, so that the meat is covered by the liquid. The meat is placed in a cool place and, if in doubt, in the refrigerator.

Step 3
Remove the meat from the liner after 48 hours and clean it. Sprinkle the dried meat with salt and pepper and fry it in a preheated pan with lots of butter until it is hot.

Step 4
Brown the onions and garlic in the pan with more butter and then add the sour cream until the colour changes.

Step 5
Add 500 ml broth and 300 ml red wine and then add mushrooms, more garlic, juniper berries and some of the spice mixture and the sauce is ready.

Step 6
The meat in a closed container for 3 hours at 160 °C. Every hour, add some of the remaining buttermilk mixture so that some liquid surrounds the meat permanently.

Step 7
After about three hours the meat is ready and can be served.

Typically, venison is eaten with dumplings

and the jam with extra pears.

Berliner Kartoffelsalat
Berlin potato salad

Working time approx. 40 minutes

Total time approx. 5 hours 10 minutes

For 4 portions

Ingredients

1 kg potatoes
15 g mustard
12 g sugar
100 ml cucumber liquid
50 ml white wine vinegar
100 ml sunflower oil
1 apple
6 gherkins
2 medium sized onions
3 cloves of garlic
Spring onion
Chives
salt and pepper

Preparation

Step 1
Boil the potatoes and then remove the skin.

Step 2
Mix mustard, sugar, cucumber water, vinegar, oil, some salt and strong pepper as well as the very finely chopped onion and garlic.

Step 3
Remove the peel from the apple and cut into small cubes. Slice the cucumber and the peeled potato and place in a bowl.

Step 4
Add the liquid from Step 2 to the bowl with the apples, cucumber and potatoes and stir until the salad appears somewhat liquid.

Step 5
Chill the salad for 3 hours and then mix with finely chopped chives and spring onions.

Klassischer Kartoffelsalat
Classic potato salad

Working time approx. 15 minutes

Total time approx. 3 hours 15 minutes

For 4 portions

Ingredients

1 kg potatoes
300 ml mayonnaise
150 g yoghurt, mild
50 g mustard
3 large gherkins
4 eggs
2 onions
salt and pepper
Cream

Preparation

Step 1
Boil potatoes and hard-boil eggs.

Step 2
Dice cucumber, eggs and onions and mix with mustard, mayonnaise and yoghurt.

Step 3
Cut the potatoes into slices and mix everything together in a large bowl.
Place in a cool place for 2 to 3 hours.

Norddeutscher Kartoffelsalat
North German potato salad

Working time approx. 40 minutes

Total time approx. 13 hours

For 4 portions

Ingredients

2 kg potatoes
150 g onions
500 ml vegetable broth
50 g mild vinegar
5 g mustard
salt and pepper
Sugar
250 g mayonnaise
5 eggs
200 g meat sausage
4 gherkins

Preparation

Step 1
Boil the potatoes and eggs, peel them, let them cool down and then cut them into thin slices.

Step 2
Cut the sausage, gherkins and onions into small pieces.

Step 3
Boil broth, vinegar and some water with mustard in a pot briefly.

Step 4
Add salt, pepper and sugar.

Step 5
Allow to cool and mix all ingredients together in a large bowl.

―――――――――――――――――――――――――――

Hühner Frikassee
Chicken fricassee

Working time approx. 40 minutes

Total time approx. 40 minutes

For 4 portions

Ingredients

1 soup chicken
3 carrot
200 g celery
150 g leek
80 g parsley
30 g butter
15 g flour
500 ml broth
(boiled chicken)
300 g pickled mushrooms
200 g pickled asparagus
300 g pickled peas
90 g pickled capers

250 ml cream
Salt

Preparation

Step 1
Boil the soup chicken in a large pot with water and salt.

Step 2
Cut all vegetables into small pieces.
Add carrots, celery, leek and parsley to the chicken.
Cook for 1 hour at medium heat.

Step 3
Remove the chicken and pluck the meat.
Cut the skin and meat smaller.
Put the skin back into the pot.
Let the pot simmer.

Step 4
Melt butter in a second pot.
Add flour and stir a lot.

Step 5
Wait until bubbles appear.

Step 6
Take 200 ml from the pot and add to the butter.

Step 7
Put the chicken, mushrooms, asparagus and part of the soup contents into the butter pot.

Stir well.

Step 8
Bring to the boil.
Add capers and cream.
Boil a little and add salt.

It can be served with rice, potatoes or toast.

Spargel mit Schweinefilet und Pilzsoße
Asparagus with pork tenderloin and mushroom sauce

Working time approx. 35 minutes

Total time approx. 1 hour 10 minutes

For 4 portions

Ingredients

1500 g asparagus, green

250 g mushrooms

1 large onion

500 g fillet of pork

40 g butter

salt and pepper

375 ml clear broth

15 g green pepper

10 g sugar

1 bunch of chervil

200 g whipped cream

30 g potato starch

Preparation

Step 1
Remove the lower third of the asparagus and peel lightly.

Step 2
Heat the butter and fry the fillet well in it. Season with salt and pepper, then remove.

Step 3
Fry the mushrooms and onions in hot frying fat. Pour in the broth and stir in the green pepper.

Step 4
Place the fillets on the mushrooms and let them simmer covered in approx. 15 - 20 minutes.

Step 5
Remove the meat from the sauce and keep warm.

Step 6
Add cream and potato starch to the mushroom sauce and stir. Bring to the boil again and season to taste.

Step 7
Cut the pork filet into slices and serve everything.

Frikadellen
Rissoles

Working time approx. 20 minutes

Total time approx. 35 minutes

For 4 portions

Ingredients

500 g minced meat
1 egg
1 onion
1 bread roll
8 g salt
4 g pepper
4 g mustard

Preparation

Step 1
Soak the roll in water and squeeze the water.

Step 2
Finely dice the onion.

Step 3
Knead all ingredients together.

Step 4
Form meatballs with moistened hands and fry in a pan with butter.

Rösti
Hash browns

Working time approx. 30 minutes

Total time approx. 30 minutes

For 4 portions

Ingredients

500 g potatoes
1 egg
30 g flour
salt and pepper
Butter

Preparation

Step 1
Peel and roughly grate the potatoes.

Step 2
Squeeze the liquid in a kitchen towel.

Step 3
Add the egg, flour, salt and pepper.

Step 4
Heat the butter in a pan and add the Rösti. Fry from both sides.

Käse-Lauchsuppe
Cheese and leek soup

Working time approx. 15 minutes

Total time approx. 45 minutes

For 4 portions

Ingredients

500 g leek
750 ml meat broth
150 g herb processed cheese
150 g cream processed cheese
1 sour cream
500 g minced beef
1 onion

Preparation

Step 1
Cut the leek into rings and cook in the broth for 20 minutes.

Step 2
Add processed cheese, sour cream.

Step 3
Cut onion into thin rings and fry in butter.

Step 4
Add meat, pepper and salt and fry until brown.

Step 5
Add the contents of the pan to the soup and stir.

It can be served with toast as a side dish.

Gulasch – Goulash

Working time approx. 30 minutes

Total time approx. 2 hours 30 minutes

For 4 portions

Ingredients

500 g goulash (beef)
Oil
1 large onion
100 g tomato paste
1 litre meat stock
salt and pepper

Preparation

Step 1
First chop the meat.

Step 2
Heat a lot of oil in a large pot.
Brown the meat strongly on all sides.

Step 3
Peel onion and cut into cubes.
Add onions to the meat.
Add tomato paste and mix.

Step 4
Add broth.
Reduce temperature.
Fry for 2 hours.
Keep water level.

Step 5
Salz und Pfeffer ergänzen.

Grüne Bohnensuppe
Green bean soup

Working time approx. 45 minutes

Total time approx. 1 hour 45 minutes

For 4 portions

Ingredients

500 g French beans
half a celery tuber
half stick leek
2 carrots
1 bunch of parsley
3 potatoes
1 vegetable stock cube
1 onion
4 g flour
4 g savory
300 g bacon or sausage

Pepper

Preparation

Step 1
Clean and chop the beans.
Clean and chop carrots, celery, parsley and leek.
Put everything into boiling salted water.
Dice bacon and add 150 g.
Cook for 30 minutes.

Step 2
Dice the potatoes. Add potatoes with stock powder, salt and pepper.
Cook for another 30 minutes.

Step 3
Brown the onions and diced bacon in a pan
with oil and add 6 g flour.

Step 4
Add the contents of the pan to the soup.

Senf-Eier
Mustard eggs

Working time approx. 15 minutes

Total time approx. 30 minutes

For 4 portions

Ingredients

8 eggs
1 onion
15 g flour
15 g butter
300 ml vegetable broth
150 ml whole milk
150 ml cream
30 g mustard
15 g sugar
salt and pepper
Soy sauce

Preparation

Step 1
Hard boil 8 eggs and cut the onion into small cubes.

Step 2
Melt the butter in a pot, then add the onions.
A few minutes later add 10 g flour.

Step 3
Remove the pan from the heat and add the vegetable stock.

Step 4
Mix everything with a whisk and place on
the stove at low temperature.

Step 5
Add milk and bring to the boil and stir several times.

Step 6
Add cream and spices and dilute with milk if desired.

Step 7
Add mustard and reduce the temperature.

Step 8
Add eggs and keep warm.

Boiled potatoes can be served with it.

Labskaus
Lobscouse

Working time approx. 25 minutes

Total time approx. 50 minutes

For 4 portions

Ingredients

300 g corned beef
750 g potatoes
3 gherkins
2 onions
50 g beetroot
salt and pepper
Allspice (ground)
Butter
50 ml cucumber liquid
4 eggs

4 matje fillets

Preparation

Step 1
Dice onions, beetroot and cucumber and chop corned beef.

Step 2
Cook the potatoes with lots of salt.

Step 3
In the meantime, fry the finely diced onions
in some fat until they are brown.

Step 4
Add corned beef and fry with lid on for about 3 minutes,
then add the gherkins with little liquid.

Step 5
Season to taste with salt, pepper and pimento and add beetroot.
Let everything simmer gently for about 10 minutes.

Step 6
Remove the skin from the potatoes and mash them slightly.

Step 7
Mix everything together and stretch with cucumber
water as required.

Serve with a fried egg and to taste with matie, bismarck
herring or rollmop.

Zwiebelkuchen
Onion cake

Working time approx. 45 minutes

Total time approx. 2 hours 30 minutes

For 4 portions

Ingredients

400 g flour

20 g yeast

250 ml water, lukewarm
4 g salt
50 g oil
800 g onions
400 g bacon (smoked)
250 g Gouda
200 g cream
2 egg yolks
Oil

Pepper

Preparation

Step 1
Dissolve the yeast in lukewarm water.

Step 2
Add flour, salt and oil and knead to a yeast dough.

Step 3
Leave covered for one hour.

Step 4
Cut onions into rings and fry in oil.

Step 5
Dice the bacon and grate the cheese.

Step 6
Mix the cream with the egg yolk.

Step 7
Roll out the dough on a sheet.
Spread the onions, add pepper.

Step 8
Mix the bacon and cheese in a bowl and also spread on the dough.

Step 9
Pour cream over it.

Step 10
Place in the oven at 50 °C.
Leave the door open and wait 15 to 20 minutes.

Step 11
Take out and put back in at 200 °C. Wait 30 minutes.

Blumenkohl & Brokkoli Auflauf
Cauliflower and Broccoli Casserole

Working time approx. 50 minutes

Total time approx. 50 minutes

For 4 portions

Ingredients

1 large cauliflower
450 g broccoli
200 g cooked ham
200 ml whipped cream
100 ml milk
200 g Gouda grated (Gouda)
50 g butter
30 g flour
salt and pepper
Nutmeg

Preparation

Step 1
Wash and chop the cauliflower and broccoli.
Dice the ham. Preheat oven to 200 °C.

Step 2
Cook the cauliflower and broccoli with salt
for 10 minutes and then drain.

Step 3
Melt butter in a pot, stir in flour and fry lightly.

Step 4
Add cream and milk slowly and stir.

Step 5
Bring to the boil. Add cheese, salt, pepper and nutmeg.

Step 6
Put the vegetables in an ovenproof dish.

Then add ham and then the sauce and sprinkle
some cheese on top.

Step 7
Place in the oven for 15 minutes.

_____

Grünkohl - Green cabbage

Working time approx. 30 minutes

Total time approx. 30 minutes

Ingredients

1500 g kale
30 g lard
2 onions chopped
30 g porridge
4 g salt
4 g mustard
4 g pepper
4 g sugar
250 ml meat broth
2 sausages (Pinkelwürste)[3]
4 coarse sausage (bratwurst)
4 smoked pork sausage[4]
250 g bacon, smoked
4 slices of Kasseler[5]

Preparation

Step 1
Remove the cabbage leaves, wash, drain and chop.

Step 2
In a large pot fry the onions in hot butter.

Step 3
Alternately add cabbage, porridge and spices.

Step 4
Add broth and boil down for 10 minutes.

Step 5
Stir everything thoroughly.

Step 6
Add bacon and smoked pork, cover and braise lightly for 90 minutes.

Step 7
Add the sausages and let them stew for 60 minutes. Finally add spices as required.

Serve traditionally with cooked potatoes.

Grünkohl – Green cabbage

Working time approx. 30 minutes

Total time approx. 12 hours 30 minutes

Ingredients

2,5 kg kale (fresh or frozen)
4 onions
60 g butter
40 g broth powder and 1 litre water
(or 1 liter of broth)
30 g mustard
10 sausages (pee)
8 Sausages (Smoked Mettwurst)
500 g bacon
8 chops (Kasseler)
Oatmeal
salt and pepper

Preparation

Step 1
Chop the onion finely and fry in a large pot with butter.

Step 2
Add the cabbage and 750 ml of hot stock.
Cook for 30 minutes.

Step 3
Remove the pellet from 3 pecks and cut into small pieces.
Add it to the cabbage.

Step 4
Add bacon and 3 pork sausages.
Simmer gently for 2 hours and stir several times.

Step 5
Remove bacon and pork sausages and place on a plate.
Add salt, pepper, mustard and stock powder.

Step 6
Refrigerate overnight.

Step 7
Heat the pot and stir more.
Add about 60 g oat flakes.
Boil until it is no longer thin.

Step 8
Put all the ingredients and all the meat in the pot and cover with broth. Warm up without boiling.

After about 20 minutes, when everything is warm, it is ready.

Potatoes can be served with it.

Grützwurst mit Kartoffelpüree
Grützwurst with mashed potatoes

Working time approx. 30 minutes

Total time approx. 55 minutes

For 4 portions

Ingredients

800 g Grützwurst[6]
1 onion(s)
30 g marjoram
15 Oil, for frying
250 ml meat brotha
Salt
Pepper
800 g pickled cabbage
15 g butter
5 juniper bearries
1 bay leaf
250 ml broth
1 large potato

Ingredients for the puree

800 g potatoes
50 ml milk
50 g butter
Salt
Nutmeg

Preparation

The Grützwurst

Step 1
Chop the onions finely. Remove the skin from the sausage and cut it into small pieces

Step 2
Lightly fry a part of the onion in oil and add the sausage.

Step 3
Add broth. Allow to simmer until the sausage is dissolved. Add salt and pepper.

The mashed potatoes

Step 4
Boil the potatoes.

Step 5
Peel and mash the potatoes.
At the same time add milk and butter. Add a little

nutmeg and mash.

The pickled cabbage

Step 6

Fry the rest of the onions with butter.

Step 7

Then add the sauerkraut, bay leaf and stock. Finally cook.

Jägerschnitzel
Hunter's Schnitzel

Working time approx. 20 minutes

Total time approx. 50 minutes

For 4 portions

Ingredients

500 g mushrooms
30 g bacon, streaky
1 onion (small diced)
125 ml vegetable broth
125 ml cream
2 g thyme
1 bunch of parsley
Milk
2 g salt
Pepper
4 pork escalope
Flour
1 egg yolk

Breadcrumbs
Butter

Preparation

Step 1
Wash the meat, dab dry and tap thinly. Season with salt and pepper.

Step 2
Beat the egg yolks.

Step 3
Turn the cutlets in flour, then in egg yolk and then in breadcrumbs.

Step 4
Fry in butter on both sides. Then take the schnitzel out of the pan.

Step 5
Cut the mushrooms into slices. Then fry for three minutes and remove from the pan.

Step 6
Chop onions and bacon finely.
Butter fry onion and bacon in a pan.

Step 7
After 5 minutes, add mushrooms, salt, pepper, thyme, broth and cream.

Step 8
Boil down for about 15 minutes and stir again and again.

Step 9

Then add milk and stir until the sauce is creamy.

Step 10

Add parsley, salt and pepper.

The schnitzel is later poured over with the sauce on the plate.

French fries are suitable for this

Kartoffelsuppe
Potato soup

Working time approx. 15 minutes

Total time approx. 35 minutes

For 4 portions

Ingredients

5 large potatoes
1 carrot
1 stick of leek
1 onion
1 litre vegetable stock
Parsley
Pepper
2 Vienna sausages
White bread
Chives
Marjoram
Bay leaves

Nutmeg

Preparation

Step 1
Clean the potatoes and carrots and cut them into cubes with the onions. Cut leek into rings.

Step 2
Fry the onions in a pot with olive oil, then add the leek. Deglaze with the vegetable stock.

Step 3
Add the potatoes, carrots and bay leaf to the stock and close the lid.
Cook for about 30 minutes.

Step 4
Fish out the bay leaf and add the herbs and puree everything.

Step 5
Add pepper, nutmeg and marjoram to taste.

Step 6
Cut the sausages into slices and add to the soup.

Step 7
Cut white bread into cubes and fry in a pan with butter.

Step 8
Pour the soup onto a plate and add the bread.

Hackbällchen mit Kartoffelspalten
Meatballs with potato wedges

Working time approx. 20 minutes

Total time approx. 1 hour 5 minutes

For 4 portions

Ingredients

250 g minced pork
250 g minced beef
1 egg
1 some breadcrumbs
salt and pepper
Paprika powder
Cayenne pepper
1 kg potato
60 g butter
Rosemary

Preparation

Step 1
Knead the minced meat with the egg, breadcrumbs and spices.

Step 2
Form small balls and place them on a baking tray.

Step 3
Peel, wash and slice the potatoes.

Step 4
Mix olive oil, rosemary, salt, paprika and cayenne pepper. Add the potatoes with it.
Pour the rest of the mixture over the balls.
Coat the meatballs with the rest of the marinade.

Step 5
Preheat oven to 180 °C

Step 6
Leave the meat and potatoes in the oven for about 40 minutes.

Leber – Liver

Working time approx. 15 minutes

Total time approx. 25 minutes

For 4 portions

Ingredients

300 g liver
1 onion
1 apple
15 g flour
15 g butter
Sugar

Preparation

Step 1

Turn the liver without fat and sinews in flour and season with pepper. Cut the apple and the onion into slices.

Step 2
Fry the liver in butter for 2 minutes on both sides. Then take it out and keep it warm.

Step 3
Add apples, onions, butter and some sugar to the pan.

Mashed potatoes are suitable for this.

Gans – Goose

Working time approx. 1 hour

Total time approx. 6 hours

———————————————————————

Ingredients

6 kg goose
15 g peppercorns
37 g sea salt
22 g sugar
8 g vegetable broth powder
5 dried apricots
1 bulb
1 apple
2 onions
6 carrots
2 oranges
450 g celeriac
Parsley
Mugwort
Marjoram
80 g parsley
150 g leek
Butter

Preparation

Step 1
Finely crush the peppercorns, salt, sugar and stock powder.

Step 2
Wash the goose, remove the fat.
Rub the goose strongly with the spice mixture inside and outside.

Step 3
Chop the apricots, pear, apple, onions, 2 carrots, oranges, celery, parsley and mugwort and mix with 15 g of the spices.
Stuff the goose with it.

Step 4
Tie the legs of the goose together.
Place the goose with the breast on a grill.

Step 5
Put 300 ml water and some butter in a pan.

Step 6
Push the grill into the oven.
Push the pan under the goose.

Step 7
Fry for 3 hours at 120 °C convection oven.

Step 8
Continue frying for 1 hour at 170 °C convection oven.

Step 9
Flip the goose.

Step 10
Fry for 1 hour at 150 °C convection oven.

Step 11
1 hour at 130 °C circulating air or grill.
Until the goose is sufficiently brown.

Step 12
Take the goose out of the oven.
Remove the stuffing.
Cut the goose.

Step 13
Place the filling around the goose as a side dish.
Pour the contents of the pan over the vegetables.

Gänsebraten
Roast goose

Working time approx. 35 minutes

Total time approx. 3 hours 35 minutes

Ingredients

about 2 kg goose (ready to roast)
salt and pepper
Mugwort
300 g plums (for baking, without stone)
300 g apple
30 g sugar
50 g brown bread (crumbled)
50 g bacon (diced)
Cornstarch
Honey
around 150 ml Beer

Preparation

Step 1
Rub goose inside and outside with salt, pepper and mugwort.

Step 2
Mix prunes, apples, sugar, bread and bacon and fill the goose with it.
Sew it up.

Step 3
Put the goose in a roasting pan and add water.
Roast the goose at 180°C for 2 hours.

Step 4
Several times pour the goose with roast stock and turn.

Step 5
Mix honey and beer. After 100 minutes brush the goose with it.

Step 6
Remove the goose from the stock and arrange the filling around it.

Served with a sauce from the stock and potatoes with red cabbage.

Krautsalat – Coleslaw

Working time approx. 30 minutes

Total time approx. 40 minutes

For 4 portions

Ingredients

750 g white cabbage
4 g salt
100 g bacon (optional)
1 onion
50 ml white wine vinegar
250 ml vegetable broth
7 g caraway (ground)
4 g mustard, hot
60 g oil
black pepper

Preparation

Step 1

Quarter the cabbage, clean, wash and cut into fine strips. Mix with salt, cover and set aside.

Step 2

Dice bacon and onion and fry briefly. Add vinegar and broth and bring to the boil and stir. Add caraway, mustard and oil.

Step 3

Mix all ingredients together, add salt and pepper.

Wirsing-Eintopf mit Kasseler
Savoy-cabbage-stew with cured pork

Working time approx. 30 minutes

Total time approx. 1 hour

For 4 portions

Ingredients

500 g cured pork
salt and pepper
1 large onion
30 g butter
1 small head of savoy cabbage
5 potatoes
4 carrots
1,5 litres of vegetable stock
1 bunch of parsley

Preparation

Step 1
Peel and chop the onion.
Wash, peel and chop the carrots and potatoes.

Step 2
Roughly chop the cabbage.
Dice the meat.

Step 3
Fry the meat with oil in a saucepan.
Add the onions and brown them.

Step 4
Add carrots, potatoes and savoy cabbage and add broth.
Add salt and pepper and bring the pot to the boil.
Simmer for 20 minutes.

Step 5
Add more salt and parsley.

Muscheln - Mussels

Working time approx. 50 minutes

Total time approx. 50 minutes

For 4 portions

Ingredients

4 kg mussel
Parsley
4 onions
300 g celeriac
2 carrots
2 leeks
2 litres of water
500 ml wine (white)
Salt
30 g black pepper
250 g butter

Preparation

Step 1
Peel and chop the vegetables, cut the onions into rings.

Step 2
Cook everything (without mussels) for 10 minutes.

Step 3
Clean the mussels and add them.
Put the lid on.

Step 4
Cook over medium heat until the mussels open. Then remove the mussels.

White bread with butter is a good side dish.

Maultaschen
Swabian raviolis

Working time approx. 50 minutes

Total time approx. 50 minutes

For 4 portions

Ingredients

For the dough
300 g flour
2 eggs
Salt
grated nutmeg
50 ml water
6 g butter

For the filling
1 onion
1 bunch of parsley
1 bread roll

15 g oil
250 g leaf spinach
250 g minced meat
0,3 g grated nutmeg
1 egg
salt and pepper

Preparation

Step 1
Knead all ingredients for the dough into a dough.

Step 2
Peel onion and chop it with parsley. Fry in a pan with oil.

Step 3
Wash, dry and chop the spinach leaves.

Step 4
Soak the roll in water. Then squeeze it out well and pluck it finely.

Step 5
Mix minced meat with egg and spices.

Step 6
Add onion, parsley, spinach and bread roll and mix.

Step 7
Roll out the pasta dough as a rectangle. Cut into small rectangles.

Step 8
Spread the mixture from Step 6 over half the dough.

Step 9
Place the other half of the dough on top.
Squeeze out the air and press the edges.
The pockets must be closed tightly.

Step 10
Cook in boiling water for about 20 minutes.

Step 11
Remove and drain.

It is recommended to eat salad with it.

Sauerbraten

marinated pot roast

Working time approx. 30 minutes

Total time approx. 8 days 2 hours 30 minutes

Ingredients

1,5 kg roast beef (from the leg)
400 ml water
250 ml red wine vinegar
250 ml red wine (dry)
3 large onions
1 carrot
80 g celeriac
3 bay leaves
4 cloves
3 grains allspice
6 grains black pepper
6 juniper berries
4 g mustard seeds
250 ml meat broth
40 g butter
15 g tomato paste
Sugar

salt and pepper
Cornstarch

Preparation

Preparation of the marinade

Step 1
Cut carrot and celery into small cubes, onions into slices.

Step 2
Mix vinegar, red wine and water as well as bay leaves, cloves, allspice seeds, peppercorns, juniper berries and mustard seeds to a marinade.

Step 3
Mix the meat, marinade and vegetables.

Step 4
The roast should be well covered with marinade.

Step 5
Place the mixture in the refrigerator for 8 days.

Preparation of the roast

Step 1
Drain the meat and place at room temperature for two hours. Rub with pepper.

Step 2
Put the marinade with spices and vegetables

on a drainer. Drain into a bowl.

Step 3
Mix 120 ml marinade (without spices and vegetables) with 250 ml hot broth.

Step 4
Melt the butter in a roaster.
Brown the meat on all sides.
Salt it.
Slowly add the marinade-broth mixture again and again.

Step 5
Add the marinade and marinade-stock mixture alternately. Turn the roast more often.

Step 6
Add vegetables, spices and tomato paste to the meat and fry.

Step 7
Cover the roaster and let it braise at 180 °C for about 3 hours.
Add marinade and stock more frequently.
Turn the roast several times.
Add hot water if necessary.

Step 8
Remove the roaster. Put the meat aside.
Add salt, pepper and red wine to the liquid.
Add hot water or cornflour.

Boiled potatoes and peas go well with it.

Ente - Duck

Working time approx. 20 minutes

Total time approx. 20 minutes

Ingredients

2 kg duck
Salt
Pepper
0,4 g caraway seeds, ground
3 carrots
2 large onions
15 g honey
15 g mustard
15 g sour cream
45 g orange liqueur

Preparation

Step 1

Clean, wash and drain the duck well.
Mix salt, pepper, caraway seeds. Rub the duck with it strongly inside and outside.

Step 2
Squeeze the duck by its wings and legs and tie up.

Step 3
Put the duck on its belly in a roaster.

Step 4
Chop the carrots and onions and put them in the roaster. Add 125 ml water.

Step 5
Put the roast in the oven.
Fry for 40 minutes at 250 °C.

Step 6
Turn the duck and fry for 80 minutes at 175 °C.
Add some hot water every 20 minutes.

Step 7
Mix honey with mustard.

Step 8
Remove the duck from the roaster and rub with honey mustard.

Step 9
Put the duck on a grill.
Fry for 15 minutes at 200 °C until crispy.

Step 10
Put 125 ml water into the roaster and boil. Add sour cream, salt and some orange liqueur.

Step 11
Stir and finish the sauce.

Best served with rice or potatoes.

Hochzeitssuppe
Wedding Soup

Working time approx. 45 minutes

Total time approx. 45 minutes

For 4 portions

Ingredients

500 g minced beef
200 g pickled asparagus
80 g leek
2 carrots
60 g parsley
200 g celeriac
5 eggs
Milk
3 litres of vegetable stock
salt and pepper
60 g chives
Cooking bag

Preparation

Step 1
Chop the carrots, leek, celery, asparagus and parsley.

Step 2
Mix the minced meat, 1 egg, salt, pepper and some chives. Form into small balls.

Step 3
Boil the broth and cook with the balls at medium temperature for about 45 minutes.

Step 4
Beat 4 eggs, salt, pepper and some parsley with a whisk.

Step 5
Place in a cooking bag, seal tightly and cook for 20 minutes.

Step 6
Remove the egg and cut into pieces.

Step 7
Add the egg pieces to the soup.

Step 8
Add pepper, salt, chives and parsley.

Recommended to be served with rice or toast.

Kohlrouladen
Cabbage rolls

Working time approx. 50 minutes

Total time approx. 1 hour 30 minutes

For 4 portions

_____

Ingredients

1000 g white cabbage
500 g minced meat
1 onion
1 bread roll, stale
1 egg
100 g bacon cubes
500 ml broth
200 ml cream
Salt
Pepper
15 g mustard
Paprika powder

Marjoram

Preparation

Step 1
Remove eight leaves from the cabbage, clean them and remove the water.
Soak the rolls and squeeze out the water.
Peel and chop the onions.

Step 2
Mix the egg, bread roll, mustard, onion, salt, pepper, marjoram and paprika powder with the minced meat.

Step 3
Spread the mixture over the cabbage leaves, roll them up and tie them together.

Step 4
Fry the roulades in a high pan and add diced bacon.

Step 5
Add broth and fry.

Step 6
Take out the roulades. Add cream to the pan. Add salt and pepper. Reduce a little.

Potatoes are suitable for this.

Eingelegte Bratheringe
Pickled fried herrings

Working time approx. 1 hour 15 minutes

Total time approx. 1 hour 15 minutes

For 4 portions

Ingredients

8 fresh herrings
750 ml white wine vinegar
750 ml water
1 lemon
200 ml oil
100 g flour
salt and pepper
3 large onions
5 bay leaves
30 g mustard seeds
15 g juniper berries

4 g pepper
60 g sugar
4 g salt
1 dried chilli pepper
2 g dill
2 g allspice
2 cloves

Preparation

Step 1
Remove the scales of the pegs, then wash and cut off heads.

Step 2
Remove water and season with lemon juice, salt and pepper.

Step 3
Turn the fish in flour and fry on both sides in oil.
Fry for about 4 minutes on each side.

Step 4
Place fish in a large bowl

Cut onions into rings.

Step 5
Boil white wine vinegar, water, sugar, salt and spices in a pot for about 5 minutes.

Step 6
Add the onion rings.
Remove the pot from the stove.

Step 7
Mix fish and marinade and place in the refrigerator for 3 days.

Step 8
Eating the herrings together with the marinade

Schupfnudeln
potato noodles

Working time approx. 30 minutes

Total time approx. 8 hours 45 minutes

For 4 portions

Ingredients

750 g potatoes
200 g flour
Salt
0,05 g grated nutmeg
1 egg
Butter
Flour

Preparation

Step 1
Boil, peel, mash and cool the potatoes.

Step 2
Knead the potatoes, some flour, salt, egg and nutmeg into a dough.
Just add a little flour every now and then. Knead until the dough no longer sticks.

Step 3
Knead the dough into noodles in the shape of a thumb. Then roll into a noodle in your hand.

Step 4
Boil them in boiling water for 3 minutes until they float.

Step 5
Skim and dry.
Place in a pan with plenty of butter and fry.

––––––––––––––––––––––––––––––––

As a side dish instead of potatoes.

Berliner Kartoffelsuppe
Berliner potato soup

Working time approx. 40 minutes

Total time approx. 30 hours 40 minutes

For 4 portions

Ingredients

2,5 kg potatoes
1 kg frozen vegetables
250 g ham or bacon (diced)
3 onions
1 kg sausages (e.g. Wiener sausage)
3 bay leaves
4 grains allspice
30 g vegetable broth (powder)
salt and pepper
80 g parsley
15 g butter

Preparation

Step 1
Peel the potatoes, cut them into small pieces, just cover them with water, salt and boil them.

Step 2
Melt the butter in a second large pot.
Add ham and bacon and fry.

Step 3
Peel and chop the onions and add.

Step 4
Add vegetables and 500 ml water.
Bring to the boil.

Step 5
Add stock powder, bay leaves, allspice and about 4 g pepper, boil and stir several times.

Step 6
When the potatoes are ready, add the water (about 3 litres) to the vegetables.
Mash the potato and add to the vegetables.

Step 7
Let the soup boil. Cut the sausages into slices and add them.

Step 8
Add pepper, salt and parsley and cook until it thickens.

Rinderrouladen
Beef roulades

Working time approx. 45 minutes

Total time approx. 45 minutes

For 4 portions

Ingredients

4 large beef roulades (600g)[7]
400 g minced meat (beef)
100 g carrots
100 g celery
2 large onions
200 g gherkins
200 g bacon (very thin)
4 g pepper, whole
1 bay leaf
2 cloves
3 grains allspice
30 g tomato paste

500 ml broth
100 ml red wine
Pepper
Salt
Sauce thickener
Oil
60 g mustard

Preparation

Step 1
Cut the gherkins into small cubes.
Cut an onion into thin rings.

Step 2
Rub the roulades on both sides with salt and pepper
and spread 15 g mustard on each.

Step 3
Spread bacon, cucumber cubes and onion rings on the roulades.
Place minced meat on each 100 g.
Roll up the roulades and tie.

Step 4
Brown the meat in a frying pan with oil.

Step 5
Cut onion, carrots and celery into small cubes.
Take the roulades out of the roaster.

Step 6
Sauté the vegetables in the roaster.
Add tomato paste and spices (cloves, allspice
seeds, peppercorns and bay leaf).

Step 7
Add the wine and stir vigorously.
Boil down the liquid.

Step 8
Add broth.
Then add roulades.

Step 9
Bring the liquid to the boil.
Then reduce the temperature and put the lid on.
Let it stew for one hour.

Step 10
Open the lid slightly.
Let it stew for another hour.

Step 11
Remove the roulades.
Sieve the sauce, add salt and pepper.

Krustenbraten
Roast crust

Working time approx. 45 minutes

Total time approx. 2 hours 45 minutes

Ingredients

2 kg pork shoulder (with rind)
1 large carrot
150 g leek
1 large onion
2 cloves of garlic
500 ml wheat beer
30 Broth powder
50 ml sour cream
Caraway seeds
salt and pepper
Butter
Cornstarch

Preparation

Step 1
Cut into the pork rind to create small cubes.
Salt the rind heavily.

Step 2
Rub the meat with caraway seeds, pepper and salt.

Step 3
Preheat the oven to 180 °C convection oven.

Step 4
Clean and chop the vegetables.
Melt butter in a roaster.

Step 5
Brown the meat strongly on all sides.
Do not sear the rind.
At the end, the rind should face upwards.

Step 6
Add the vegetables.
Add 200 ml beer and bring to the boil.

Step 7
Add the stock powder and water.
The meat should be half covered with water.

Step 8
Place in the oven for 2 hours.
Add beer and water from time to time.

Step 9
Take meat out of the roaster.
Separate the liquid from the vegetables.
Pour liquid into a pot. Put the vegetables back into the roaster.

Step 10
Place the meat on the vegetables and put it back in the oven.

Step 11
Add the remaining beer to the sauce and bring to the boil. Add 30 g sour cream and stir.
Reduce temperature.
Add cornflour if necessary.

Set the oven to grill mode for 2 minutes.

Step 12
Cut the meat into thin slices and serve with the vegetables.

Potatoes or dumplings are suitable for this.

Schweinshaxen
Knuckles of pork

Working time approx. 15 minutes

Total time approx. 2 hours 45 minutes

For 4 portions

Ingredients

2000 g pork knuckle
2 onions
5 cloves of garlic
1 carnation
5 bay leaves
8 juniper berries
2 g caraway seeds
8 g salt
Pepper

Preparation

Step 1
Chop onion and garlic finely.

Step 2
Boil water in a large pot.
Add onions, garlic and the spices.

Step 3
Put knuckles in the water.
(They should be covered with water).
Simmer for about 90 minutes.

Step 4
Place the meat in the oven at 180 °C for one hour.

Pilz-Sahnesoße
Mushroom cream sauce

Working time approx. 20 minutes

Total time approx. 20 minutes

For 4 portions

Ingredients

60 g butter for frying
1 onion
1 clove of garlic
Salt
Pepper
Nutmeg
200 g mushrooms
50 ml white wine
40 g parsley
10 g broth
30 g butter for the roux
15 g flour

200 g cream
Half a lemon (take the juice)

Preparation

Step 1
Chop the onions and garlic finely and fry in a pan with butter.

Step 2
Cut the mushrooms into slices and add lemon juice.

Step 3
Add mushrooms, pepper, nutmeg and salt to the onions.

Step 4
When everything is done, deglaze with white wine and add stock powder.
Chop parsley and add.

Step 5
Melt butter in a pot and add flour.
Stir with a whisk and let it brown.

Step 6
Add cream and allow to thicken
Supplement with milk or flour.

Step 7
Add the contents of the pan and stir.
Simmer for 10 minutes.

Linsen mit Würstchen
Lentils with sausages

Working time approx. 20 minutes

Total time approx. 1 hour 5 minutes

For 4 portions

Ingredients

1 onion
80 g leek
1 carrot
80 g celeriac
150 g dried lentils
150 g belly meat
500 ml vegetable broth
1 potato
4 sausages
30 g butter
salt and pepper
Nutmeg

30 g red wine vinegar
250 g spaetzle

Preparation

Step 1
Dice celeriac and onion, cut leek and carrot into rings and grate potato finely.

Step 2
Brown the onion and bacon, then add the vegetables (without potatoes).
Then add the lenses.

Step 3
Add lentils and broth.
Cook for 10 minutes.

Step 4
Add the potatoes.
Cook until the lentils are done.

Step 5
Add spices and vinegar.

Step 6
Cook the sausages lightly.

Spätzle are suitable for this.

Brezeln - Pretzels

Working time approx. 45 minutes

Total time approx. 3 hours 5 minutes

For 4 portions

Ingredients

500 g wheat flour
300 ml milk
4 g salt
42 g fresh yeast
4 g sugar
40 g butter
Salt
1 litre of water
50 g baking soda

Preparation

Step 1
Mix the yeast with sugar and very little milk.
Leave to stand for 30 minutes.

Step 2
Then knead with salt, flour, the remaining milk and 40 g butter.
Keep warm for 40 minutes.

Step 3
Spread the flour on a work surface.
Place the dough on top and knead.
Form a roll.

Step 4
Divide the dough into 16 pieces
Roll a 30 cm long rod from each piece.
Each bar should be a little thicker in the middle.

Step 5
Now form the pretzel.
1. First form a "U".
2. wrap the U-arms together
3. press the arms onto the pretzel

Step 6
Let the pretzels stand for 20 minutes.

Step 7
In the fridge for an hour.

Step 8
Boil about 1 litre of water.
Add baking soda very slowly.

Step 9
Take the pretzels out of the fridge and cook
them one by one for 30 seconds.

Step 10

Sprinkle coarse salt over the pretzels.

Step 11

Rub the baking tray with lots of butter.
Place the pretzels on top.
Put them in the oven

Step 12

Set the oven to 220 °C.
Bake for 20 minutes.

_____

Semmelknödel Dumplings

Working time approx. 20 minutes

Total time approx. 40 minutes

For 4 portions

Ingredients

6 rolls (buns)
50 g parsley, chopped
10 g butter
1 onion
250 ml milk
3 eggs
salt and pepper
Breadcrumbs

Preparation

Step 1
Chop onions, bread rolls and parsley

Step 2
Briefly fry the parsley and onion with butter in a pot.
Then mix with the bread roll.

Step 3
Heat the milk in another pot to a high temperature.
Then pour the milk into the other pot.
Let it simmer for 10 minutes.

Step 4
Mix salt, pepper and the eggs.
Then add them.

Step 5
Stir a firm dough.
Add breadcrumbs if necessary.

Step 6
Form balls from the dough. Big as a tennis ball.

Step 7
Boil water with salt and put the balls in for 20 minutes.
The water should then no longer boil.

Step 8
When the balls have risen, take them out of the pot.

Step 9
Serve as a side dish.

Impressum

The German Kitchen
Theaterstraße 8
37073 Göttingen

and

Mindful Publishing
by
TTENTION Inc.
Wilmington - DE19806
Trolley Square 20c

All rights reserved

Instagram: mindful_publishing
Contact: mindful.publishing@web.de

Helping you to a healthier lifestyle

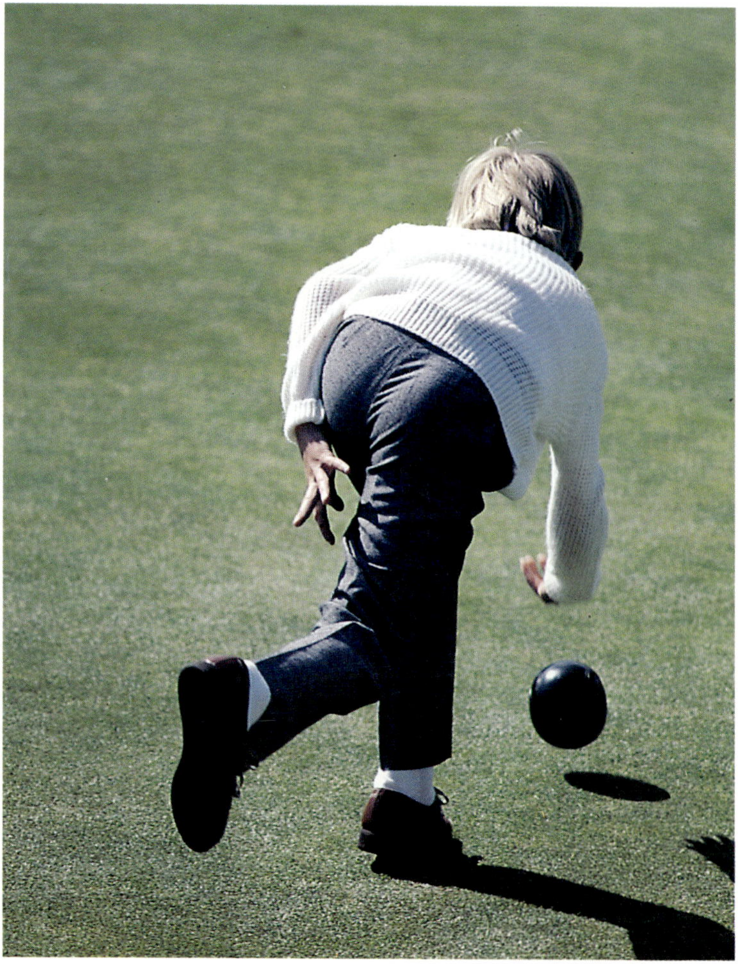

Contents

Introduction	5
Eat well, be well	6
Starch and fibre	8
Fats, salt and sugar	10
Are you a healthy weight?	16
Food labelling	19
Know your drink	22
Physical activity	26
Coping with stress	30
Smoking	34
Look after your heart	38
Further information	42
Further reading and viewing	45

4

Introduction

Everyday decisions and everyday habits can affect our health now, and in the future. Not all illness and disease is preventable but a large proportion of early deaths in the UK, particularly from coronary heart disease, could be avoided. Doctors and scientists are in agreement on the issues which can affect our health, and on the steps we can take to improve it.

Healthy living, however, does not mean giving up all the things you enjoy doing, eating or drinking, or having to don a tracksuit and jog for hours. Small changes can make a big difference!

This book aims to give you plenty of ideas to try and gives advice on how to get started.

Whatever you decide to do though, remember not to try and do everything at once. Start slowly with small changes and as you find they fit into your everyday routine then you can try further ideas. Keep an eye on your own progress and see how well you are doing. In time these small changes will be so firmly established in your lifestyle that they will be the natural way to continue.

Eat well, be well

Your daily choice of foods is important to your health. If you are choosing food for your family, you have also got their health in your hands. Choose the right food for your body – a varied diet will provide you with the nutrients you need.

Guidelines for a healthy diet

- Enjoy your food.
- Eat a variety of foods.
- Eat the right amount to be a healthy weight.
- Eat plenty of foods rich in starch and fibre.
- Don't eat too much fat.
- Don't eat sugary foods too often.
- Keep an eye on the vitamins and minerals in your food.
- If you drink alcohol, keep within sensible limits.

If you follow these eight guidelines you are likely to have a healthy diet but above all, it is important to enjoy food. All foods provide you with some nutrients and add variety, but some foods should not be eaten too often or in large quantities if you want to be sure of enjoying good health.

Starch and fibre

Starchy foods are filling without providing too many calories. They are also a good source of nutrients like protein, and some minerals and vitamins. They should form the main part of most meals. The wholegrain varieties of starchy foods are a particularly good choice because they are high in fibre. Fibre is found only in foods that come from plants like cereals, beans, peas, vegetables and fruit. Animal products like meat, cheese, or eggs contain no fibre at all.

Starch and fibre can:
- give a satisfying feeling of fullness without too many calories;
- help to prevent constipation and other disorders of the bowel, gallstones, and possibly bowel cancer;
- possibly help to keep blood cholesterol level down, which is important in reducing the risk of heart disease.

Eat more starch and fibre

■ Eat more bread – especially wholemeal breads. Chapattis are a good choice.

■ Eat more potatoes. Try baking or boiling them, instead of having them chipped or roasted.

■ Sweet potatoes, cassava, and plantain are also good choices.

■ Try dishes based on rice or pasta, particularly brown rice and wholewheat pasta.

■ Eat plenty of raw or lightly cooked vegetables – also fresh fruit and salads.

Good sources of starch and fibre are:

Bread	Breakfast cereals
Chapattis	Maize
Millet	Pasta
Potatoes	Plantains, green bananas
Rice	Flour and flour products

To further increase fibre in the diet, choose:

Vegetables	Fruit
Beans, peas and lentils	

Fats, salt and sugar

Some types of fat are essential for good health, but we eat far more fat than we need. Eating too much fat is linked to heart disease, and might lead to becoming overweight. Taking too much salt may also increase the risk of heart disease in some people. Sugar gives us energy, but no useful nutrients. By cutting down on all of them, we can begin to eat more healthily.

Fat

There are two types of fat:

■ **Saturated fats (or saturates)**

Saturates are found mainly in meat and meat products (beef, lamb, pork, suet, lard, dripping); in dairy products (milk, butter, cream, cheese); in hard margarines, in cooking fat; and in cakes, biscuits, puddings, and chocolate. These fats may appear on the ingredients list of a product as 'hydrogenated vegetable fat/oil'.

■ **Unsaturated fats (or unsaturates)**

Unsaturates include polyunsaturated fats and monounsaturated fats. They are found in vegetable oils such as sunflower, corn and soya, rape-seed, and olive oils; in soft margarines labelled 'high in polyunsaturates'; in nuts; and in oily fish like herring, mackerel, tuna, pilchards, sardines, and trout.

The more saturates you eat, the higher your blood cholesterol is likely to be. It is a high level of blood cholesterol that increases your risk of developing heart disease. Over time, cholesterol can build up on the walls of the arteries, especially those around the heart, and can lead to a heart attack or heart disease. In the UK, heart disease is the cause of nearly a third of early deaths in men of working age.

How to cut down on fat

For good health it is important to reduce the total amount of fat you eat. When you do eat fats, **choose those high in unsaturates.**

■ Use skimmed or semi-skimmed milk rather than whole milk.

■ Choose the leanest cuts of meat you can afford, and trim off all the visible fat.

■ Eat more fish and poultry with the skin removed.

■ Meat products like pies, sausages, corned beef, and salami can be very high in fat.

■ Grill, microwave, steam, poach, or boil your food rather than fry it. Drain off excess fat.

■ Choose a low-fat spread or margarine labelled high in polyunsaturates rather than butter, hard margarine, or ordinary soft margarine.

■ Cut down on crisps, chocolate, cakes, pastries, and biscuits.

■ If you like cheese, go for low-fat varieties such as half-fat hard cheese and cottage cheese.

Salt

We need only about 3 grams of salt each day (half a teaspoonful), but on average we eat about 13 grams (2½ teaspoonfuls) a day. About two-thirds of this comes from processed foods. Of the remainder about half is added during cooking or at the table, and half is naturally present in food. For some people, too much salt may lead to high blood pressure, which in turn increases the risk of strokes and heart disease. But everyone should play it safe and cut down on the amount of salt we eat.

How to reduce your salt intake

■ Gradually reduce the amount of salt you add in cooking, and flavour your food with lemon juice, herbs, or spices.

■ Cut down on snacks with a high salt content, such as crisps and salted nuts.

■ Taste your food before adding salt. Try to get out of the habit of adding salt to food at the table.

■ Cut down on salted foods such as meat pies, bacon, gammon, sausages, cheese, and shellfish in brine.

■ Look for products labelled 'low salt' or 'no added salt' such as tinned vegetables and soups.

Sugar

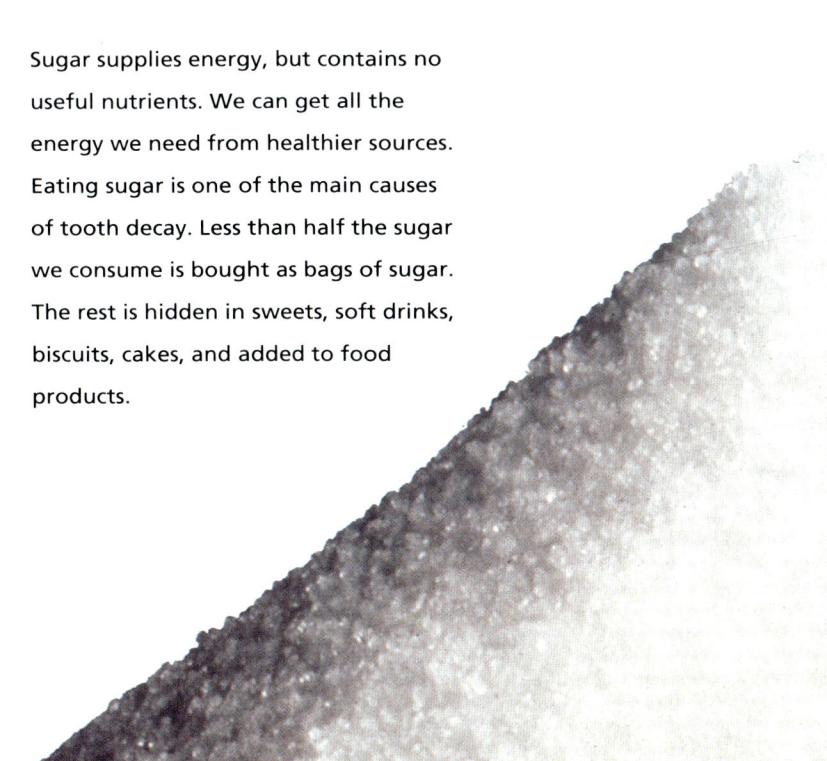

Sugar supplies energy, but contains no useful nutrients. We can get all the energy we need from healthier sources. Eating sugar is one of the main causes of tooth decay. Less than half the sugar we consume is bought as bags of sugar. The rest is hidden in sweets, soft drinks, biscuits, cakes, and added to food products.

Facts on sugar

- Eating sugary foods and drinks is the main cause of tooth decay, especially when eaten throughout the day. When you eat sugary foods, the sugar starts a chemical reaction in your mouth. The bacteria on your teeth use sugar to produce acid, which attacks the enamel on your teeth. This can lead to tooth decay.

- Table sugar gives you calories with no other nutrients: no vitamins, no minerals, no protein.

- Some people find the taste of sugar pleasant, so we may eat more food and calories than we really need. This may lead to weight gain. Many sugary foods also contain a lot of fat.

- In Britain, we buy on average 44kg (97lb) of sugar per year.

How to cut down on sugar

- Read food labels carefully, and buy products which contain less sugar. Watch out for sucrose, glucose, dextrose, fructose, and maltose on the ingredients list of packaged food – they are all forms of sugar. Honey, syrup, raw sugar, brown sugar, cane sugar, and muscovado are other forms of sugar you may come across.

- Try to limit your intake of sugary foods and drinks to meal-times.

- Try drinking tea and coffee without sugar. You might find it easier to cut down a little at a time.

- Choose low-calorie soft drinks, or unsweetened fruit juices diluted with water or soda-water.

- Try halving the sugar you use in your recipes. (This works for most things except jam, meringues, and ice-cream.)

- Beware of sweets, cereal bars, and chocolate.

- Avoid sugar-coated breakfast cereals.

Are you a healthy weight?

Food provides energy (or calories) which your body needs to grow and work properly. If the foods you eat provide more energy than you use then you will put on weight. Equally, if you don't eat enough you will become underweight.

Are you the right weight for your height?

The information on this chart is designed for adult men and women only.
Make a straight line up from your weight (without clothes), and a line across from your height (without shoes). Put a mark where the two lines meet. This tells you whether you need to lose or gain weight.

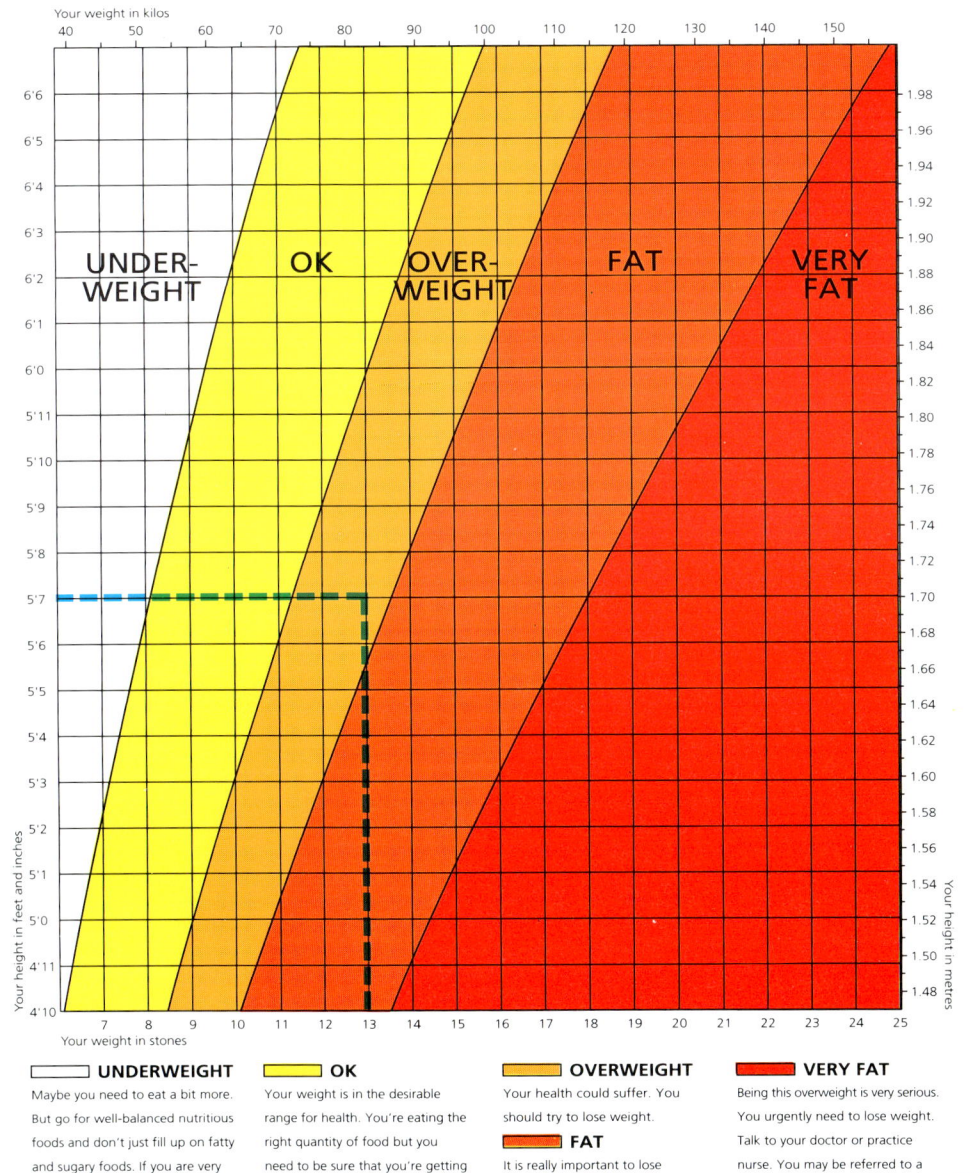

[Weight/height chart with zones: UNDER-WEIGHT, OK, OVER-WEIGHT, FAT, VERY FAT. X-axis: weight in kilos (40–150) and stones (7–25). Y-axis: height in feet and inches (4'10" – 6'6") and metres (1.48 – 1.98).]

UNDERWEIGHT
Maybe you need to eat a bit more. But go for well-balanced nutritious foods and don't just fill up on fatty and sugary foods. If you are very underweight, see your doctor about it.

OK
Your weight is in the desirable range for health. You're eating the right quantity of food but you need to be sure that you're getting a healthy balance in your diet.

OVERWEIGHT
Your health could suffer. You should try to lose weight.

FAT
It is really important to lose weight.

VERY FAT
Being this overweight is very serious. You urgently need to lose weight. Talk to your doctor or practice nurse. You may be referred to a dietitian.

For example, a person who is 5'7 tall and weighs 13 stones is overweight.

Overweight?

If the foods you are eating are providing more energy (calories) than you are using, then you will gain weight. To lose weight, you need to **increase** the amount of exercise you take, and **decrease** the amount of calories you consume from food and drink. By doing this you will use up more energy (calories) and begin to lose weight.

■ Would it be fun to walk around all day with 14 bags of sugar strapped to your waist? If you are 14kg (2.2st) overweight that is what you are doing. Is it any wonder you tire easily and become breathless?

■ Carrying extra weight puts a strain on the weight-bearing joints, especially the knees and hips. It also increases the risk of heart disease, high blood pressure, diabetes, and gall bladder disease.

■ People often believe that as you get older you automatically get fatter. This is not true. If you are gaining weight, it means that the balance between what you eat and the energy you use has changed. By increasing your physical activity and eating sensibly you can help restore the balance.

■ By following the healthy-eating suggestions in this booklet, rather than going on a crash diet, you will be eating a balanced diet, with all the nutrients you need.

Food labelling

The law requires that food labels provide detailed information about what the food is and what its ingredients are. Many manufacturers are also beginning to meet the public's demand for more information about the nutritional content of food. This allows comparisons to be made between similar foods and for lower fat and lower sugar varieties to be chosen.

The label

Most pre-packaged food labels must show:
- the name of the food,
- a list of ingredients in order of weight,
- how long it can be kept and how to store it,
- the weight, volume, or number in the pack,
- how to cook or prepare it,
- the name and address of the maker, packager, or seller,
- sometimes, the place of origin.

Nutritional information, though not required by law, is provided by many manufacturers. Use these labels to compare similar foods to help you choose the lower fat and the lower sugar varieties.

This sort of label tells you how much of certain nutrients the food contains.

NUTRITION INFORMATION

100 g (3½ oz) GIVES YOU

Energy	1475 kJ	350 kcal
Protein		11.4 g
Carbohydrate		70.3 g
of which sugars		1.0 g
Fat		3.4 g
of which saturates		0.5 g
Sodium		0.2 g
Fibre		9.5 g

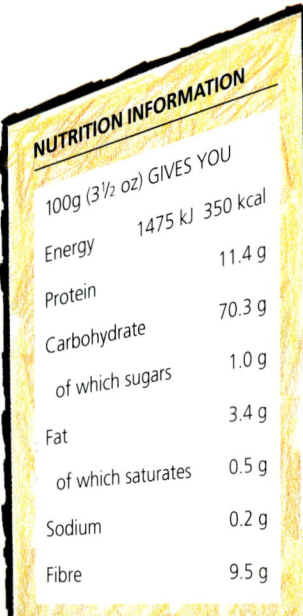

kJ or kilojoules, is a modern measure of energy.

This figure tells you the calories or energy in 100 g of the product.

Carbohydrates are a major source of energy. They include sugar and starch. We need to watch our sugar intake and try to eat more starchy carbohydrates. If there is a separate figure given for sugars, you can work out whether the carbohydrates in the product are mostly sugar or starch. Here they are mostly starch.

This figure tells you how much saturated fat there is in 100 g of the product. Try to buy foods with a low amount of saturated fat.

Sodium levels give you an idea of how much salt is in the food. The higher the figure, the more salt there is.

This figure tells you how much fibre there is in the food.

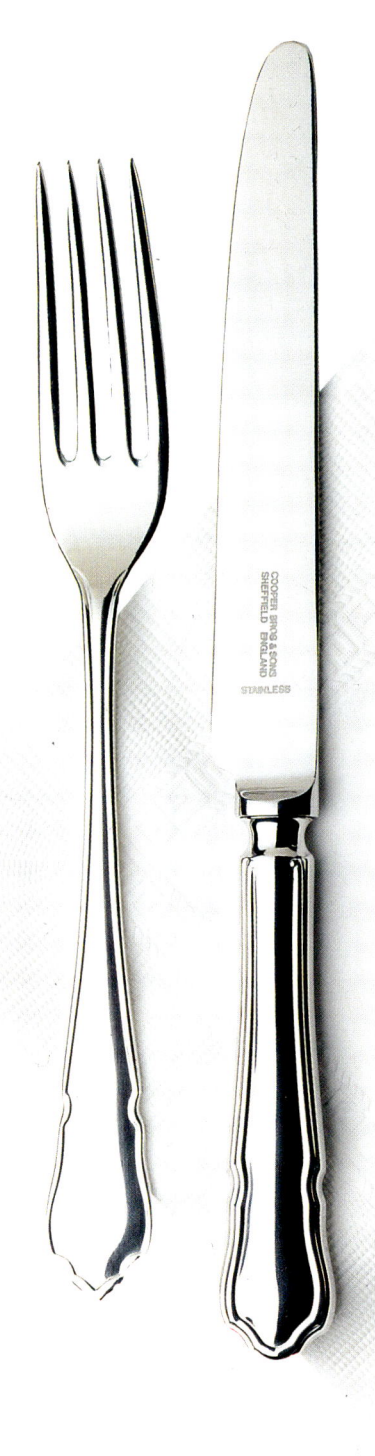

Know your drink

For many people drinking alcohol is a pleasant social activity. But drinking too much or drinking at the wrong time can cause problems – and not only for the drinker.

How much alcohol?

There's the same amount of alcohol in a single whisky as there is in half a pint of beer, a glass of wine, or a glass of sherry. Each of these measures represents one unit of alcohol.

What is a sensible limit?

For men

No more than 21 units a week spread throughout the week with one or two drink-free days.

For women

No more than 14 units a week spread throughout the week with one or two drink-free days.

Regular drinking in excess of these levels increases the risks to your health. Drinking alcohol on inappropriate occasions, or binge-drinking, can lead to accidents. In particular, drinking should be avoided before driving.

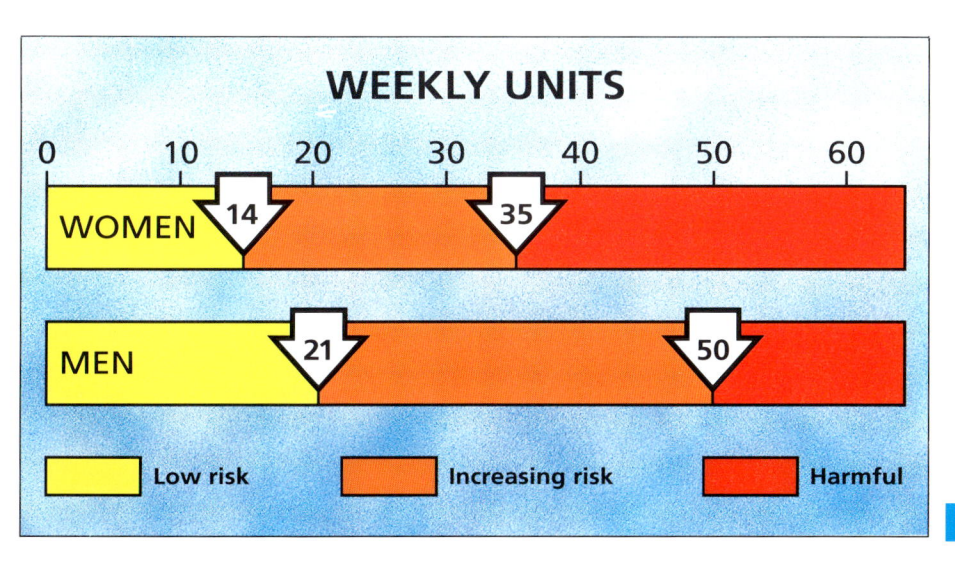

WEEKLY UNITS

WOMEN: 14, 35
MEN: 21, 50

Low risk | Increasing risk | Harmful

Young and elderly people are more at risk and should drink less. If you are taking certain types of medicine or driving then don't drink at all. If you are pregnant the best advice is to cut down to 1 or 2 units once or twice a week or to give up completely.

Low-alcohol and alcohol-free drinks

If you need to or want to cut down on your drinking, you could switch to low-alcohol or alcohol-free drinks. A pint of strong lager can contain as much as 4 units of alcohol, while most pints of low-alcohol lagers have less than 1 unit. (See the **How many units is your drink?** chart.)

Remember, home measures are usually much more than pub measures.

1 unit of alcohol is equal to ½ PINT ORDINARY BEER, LAGER OR CIDER **or** ⅓ PINT OF STRONG BEER, LAGER OR CIDER **or** ONE SMALL GLASS OF SHERRY

How many units are in your drink?

Beers and lagers	Units
1 pint of Export beer	2½
1 can* of Export beer	2
1 pint of ordinary beer or lager	2
1 can* of ordinary beer or lager	1½
1 pint of strong ale or lager	4
1 can* of strong ale or lager	3
1 pint of extra-strong beer or lager	5
1 can* of extra-strong beer or lager	4

Ciders	
1 pint of cider	3
1 pint of strong cider	4

Spirits	
1 standard single measure	1
1 standard single measure in Northern Ireland	1½

Table wine	
1 small glass	1

Sherry	
1 standard small measure	1

Low-alcohol

Low-alcohol beers, lagers, ciders, and wines vary enormously in alcohol content. Some wines are as much as half the strength of ordinary table wine while beers, lagers, and ciders listed are one third of ordinary strength, but all can be as low as 0.05 per cent – virtually alcohol free.

Low-alcohol lagers and beers	Units
Half-pint	⅓
1 pint	⅔
1 can*	½

Low-alcohol cider	
Half-pint	⅓
1 pint	½

(*1 can = 16 fl oz = 440ml = ¾ pint).

ONE SMALL GLASS OF WINE

ONE SINGLE MEASURE OF SPIRITS

Physical activity

Physical activity or exercise does not have to be exhausting or painful to be good for you, but it should be regular. Whatever your age, physical activity plays an important part in your health and general well-being.

The benefits

- Regular physical activity helps you to feel good.
- It helps your heart to work more efficiently, improves your circulation, and helps to protect against heart disease.
- It helps you control your weight.
- It keeps your neck, back, and joints supple, so you are more mobile as you get older.
- It tones flabby muscles and gives you extra strength.
- It helps you to relax.

Try to choose activities that:

- you enjoy,
- make you feel good,
- can be done regularly,
- fit easily into your everyday routine.

Start today!

- Choose an activity you enjoy and build up your fitness gradually. A good start would be to use the stairs instead of taking the lift, or try getting off the bus one stop earlier and finishing your journey on foot.
- Aim to exercise for 20 to 30 minutes, two or three times each week.
- Make sure you take some form of exercise every day. A brisk walk is an excellent way to start.

Gently does it

- If you do not already exercise regularly, start gently and gradually increase the amount.
- Do not try vigorous, competitive games until you reach an adequate level of fitness. To begin with try swimming, cycling, gardening, or dancing.
- If you feel unwell, do not exercise until you feel better.

The S factors

For all-round fitness you need stamina, suppleness, and strength.

While there are hundreds of activities to choose from, the benefits to be gained from each will vary. The benefits gained from swimming, for example, are not the same as those gained from weight-lifting.

This is why knowing about the S factors is useful.

Stamina

This is necessary for staying power – that is, your ability to keep going without gasping for breath. Improving your stamina will enable you to cope more easily with prolonged exertion. Choosing activities that increase your stamina helps to protect you against heart disease.

Suppleness

This is the ability of your joints to move through a full range of movement. Suppleness means being able to bend, stretch, twist, and turn. If you are supple you will be able to be more active as you get older.

Strength

This is being able to exert force for pushing, pulling, and lifting, which need strong shoulder, trunk, and leg muscles. Strong trunk muscles will also help to give you good posture.

Look at the guide below to see which activities give you the three S's. For all-round fitness, choose those with the most squares.

Activities	Stamina	Suppleness	Strength
Badminton	■■	■■	■■
Climbing stairs	■■	■	■■
Cricket	■	■■	■
Cycling (hard)	■■■	■■	■■■
Dancing (ballroom)	■	■■■	■
Dancing (disco)	■■	■■■	■
Gardening (digging)	■■	■■	■■■
Football (soccer)	■■	■■	■■
Golf	■	■■	■
Hill walking	■■	■	■■
Housework	■	■■	■
Jogging	■■■	■■	■■
Mowing the lawn	■	■	■■
Squash	■■	■■	■■
Swimming (hard)	■■■	■■■	■■■
Tennis	■	■■	■
Walking (briskly)	■■	■	■
Weight-lifting	■	■	■■■
Yoga	■	■■■	■

Legend:
- ■ No real effect
- ■■ Beneficial effect
- ■■■ Very good effect
- ■■■■ Excellent effect

This table should be used only as a rough guide. A great deal will depend on how much effort is put into the activity.

Before you start – some sensible precautions

There are few risks in regular, rhythmic, physical activity as long as you choose the right activity, begin gently, and work up gradually.

Most people do not need a medical examination before taking exercise. However, if you have high blood pressure, heart disease, chest trouble (like asthma or bronchitis), joint pains, serious illness, or if you're recovering from an operation, do consult your doctor about the best form of activity for you.

If you have **any** of these symptoms while doing an activity:

- Pain
- Unusual fatigue
- Dizziness
- Feel sick or unwell

STOP THE ACTIVITY!

If the symptoms are persistent, or come back later, or if you're worried about them, see your doctor.

Where to go

If you want to take up a new activity, drop into your library or sports centre and look at the noticeboards or leaflets. Also look in your local newspaper to see what is going on in your area. Join a 'Look after your Heart: Look after Yourself' course (see p. 42).

Walking is the most natural activity of all, and a good way to get started on your exercise programme.

Coping with stress

Your body's response to stress prepares it for action. Thousands of years ago, if primitive man was attacked by a wild animal his stress reaction would help him either to run away or to defend himself by fighting. This is known as the 'fight-or-flight' response.

However, this stress response is less useful to us in modern-day stressful situations because the body is frequently preparing itself for action that does not occur.

Reactions to stress

When a person is under stress, the body can react in the following ways:

- muscles tense
- blood pressure rises
- breathing becomes faster and shallower
- the liver releases sugar, cholesterol, and fatty acids into the blood
- adrenaline flow increases
- sweating increases
- immune responses decrease
- digestion slows down
- feelings of anger or anxiety arise

A certain amount of stress can spur you on to get things done. But if your body is subjected to stress for long periods of time, this can seriously damage your health.

Some effects of stress

The effects of stress can take many forms:

- poor sleep
- restlessness, tension
- anxiety
- frustration, feelings of helplessness
- exhaustion
- inappropriate aggression, irritability
- over- or under-eating
- loss of self-esteem
- feelings of loneliness or isolation
- over-stimulation and excitability
- palpitations
- lack of concentration

Disorders in which stress may play a part

- **Migraine / headache**
- **Muscular tension**

Backache

Stiff neck and shoulders

Aches and pains

- **Cardiovascular disorders**

High blood pressure

Heart attack

Stroke

- **Respiratory disorders**

Asthma

- **Digestive disorders**

Peptic ulcers

Irritable bowel syndrome

Constipation

Diarrhoea

- **Mental disorders**

Depression

Anxiety

Nervous breakdown

- **Accidents**
- **Poor sleeping habits**
- **Cancer**

Simple steps to coping with stress

Try to:

- work out exactly what it is making you feel stressed;
- organise your time by making a list of what is most and what is least urgent, and do things in that order; don't take on more than you can cope with;
- take regular exercise – gentle, rhythmic exercise like swimming, walking or jogging is a superb way of releasing tension caused by stress;
- avoid harmful ways of coping with stress such as drinking, smoking or compulsive eating (they may seem to relieve stress, but in the long run they add to it and lead to poor health);
- learn to relax – look for 'Look after Yourself' classes in your area which will show you a variety of simple relaxation techniques (see p. 44).

Try to relax

Learn to recognise when your muscles are tensed; feel the tension with your fingertips.

Try the following to help you relax:

1. Sit with your feet flat on the floor, or lie in a comfortable and supported position. Rest your hands lightly on your thighs.

2. Put one hand on your chest and the other on your stomach and breathe slowly and deeply through your nose.

If you are breathing correctly, your stomach, not your chest, should rise at the start of each breath.

3. As you breathe, gradually drop your shoulders and relax your hands. Make sure your teeth are not tightly clenched.

It takes time to learn, but when you are able to practise calm, controlled breathing, and are able to release unnecessary muscular tension at will during the day, you will have developed a very useful technique for combating stressful moments in your life.

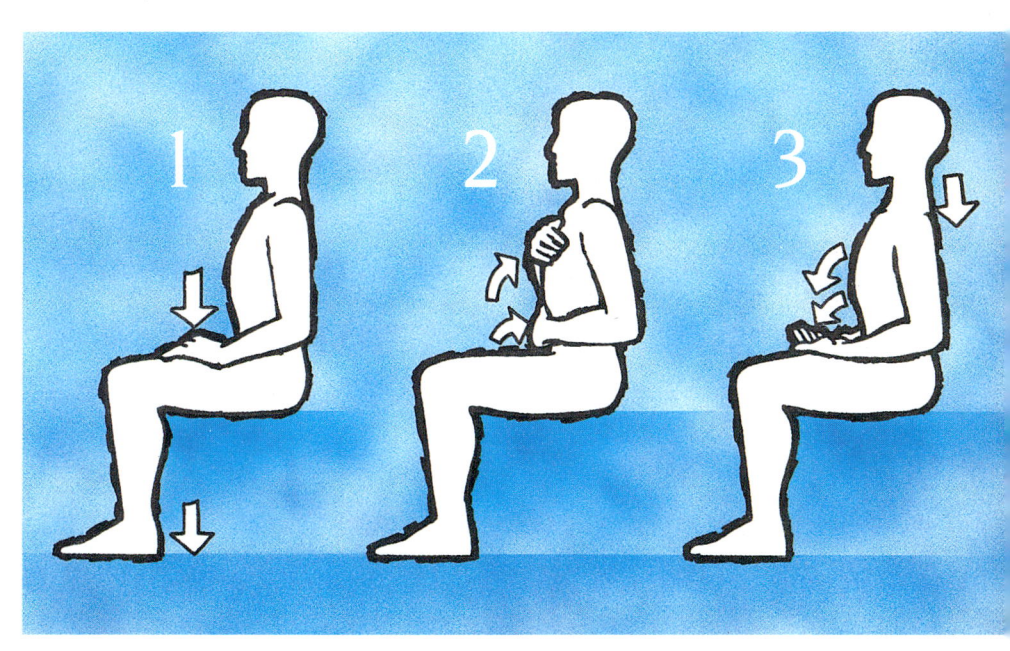

Smoking

Giving up smoking is the most important step people can take to improve their health. If you are a smoker, then take heart – over ten million people in the UK have successfully given up!

Smoking facts

Did you know that:

■ About 100,000 people in the UK are killed by smoking each year.

■ Most of these deaths are due to one of the three main diseases associated with cigarette smoking: coronary heart disease, destructive lung disease (including bronchitis and emphysema), and lung cancer.

■ A smoker runs two to three times the risk of having a heart attack as a non-smoker.

■ Approximately nine out of ten deaths from lung cancer and bronchitis are caused by smoking.

■ Non-smokers who live or work with smokers are at greater risk of lung cancer and some other diseases.

■ Smoking can lead to bad breath, staining and yellowing of teeth, shortness of breath, and addiction to nicotine.

Smoking is anti-social. As well as causing annoyance by making hair and clothes smell unpleasant, exposure to other people's smoke can cause eyes to hurt, headaches, coughs, sore throat, dizziness, and nausea.

Breathing in other people's smoke is called **'passive smoking'**. Regular exposure to passive smoking can increase a non-smoker's risk of getting lung cancer by 10 to 30 per cent.

The children of parents who smoke are more likely to be admitted to hospital for bronchitis and pneumonia in the first year of life.

Stopping smoking made easier

Stopping smoking may be easier than you think. Over 10 million people in Britain have stopped smoking and stayed stopped in the last 15 years, that's over 1000 every day!

Stopping smoking can be broken down into three stages.

■ Stage one, preparing to stop, can take anything from days to months but it is the most important stage. If the preparation is right, you will succeed.

■ The second stage is stopping.

■ The third stage is staying stopped.

Many smokers go through the first two stages several times before eventually succeeding. It's a little like going round in a revolving door several times before leaving it. So if you don't succeed the first time don't worry. Try again. Eventually you will succeed.

Are you ready to stop?

The first part of preparing is thinking about stopping. Ask yourself 'Do I really want to stop?' and look at all the things holding you back. Are they real problems or just excuses (perhaps both)? To succeed in stopping *you* must really *want* to stop, and not just do it for someone else. Do you want to improve your health? Set an example to children? Have more money to spend? Get rid of nicotine stains? Conquer the addiction? Or stop for some other personal reason?

Go over all the barriers to stopping and make sure they are not just excuses to put it off. Make sure you have all the information you need – about how dangerous smoking is, about the benefits of stopping, and about how not to put on weight when you stop. All of these are dealt with in the Health Education Authority booklet *Stopping smoking made easier* (see p. 45).

Once you really want to stop, and are determined to succeed, you are ready to draw up an action plan.

Stopping

Choose a day to stop. Ask your family and friends for help and understanding. Get rid of your cigarettes the day before, and plan rewards, especially at the end of the first day, week, and month.

The key to your success is to understand your habit, anticipate problems, and plan ahead. Work out the situations that are going to be difficult and have a strategy for dealing with them. Have a plan to get through day one. This could include keeping busy, chewing gum or something else non-fattening, drinking juice (Vitamin C helps get rid of the nicotine) and being careful with alcohol.

Staying stopped

You stay stopped by applying these principles on a day-by-day basis, and by not playing games, like having 'just one' to prove you're in control now. And try to take one day at a time. It will make the whole task more manageable. The benefits of stopping start immediately, and after a month most smokers will have got over the worst of the withdrawal.

You might also think about using treatment aids – including tablets and lozenges – available from your pharmacist. These include nicotine chewing gum and patches, which can be helpful if the instructions are followed.

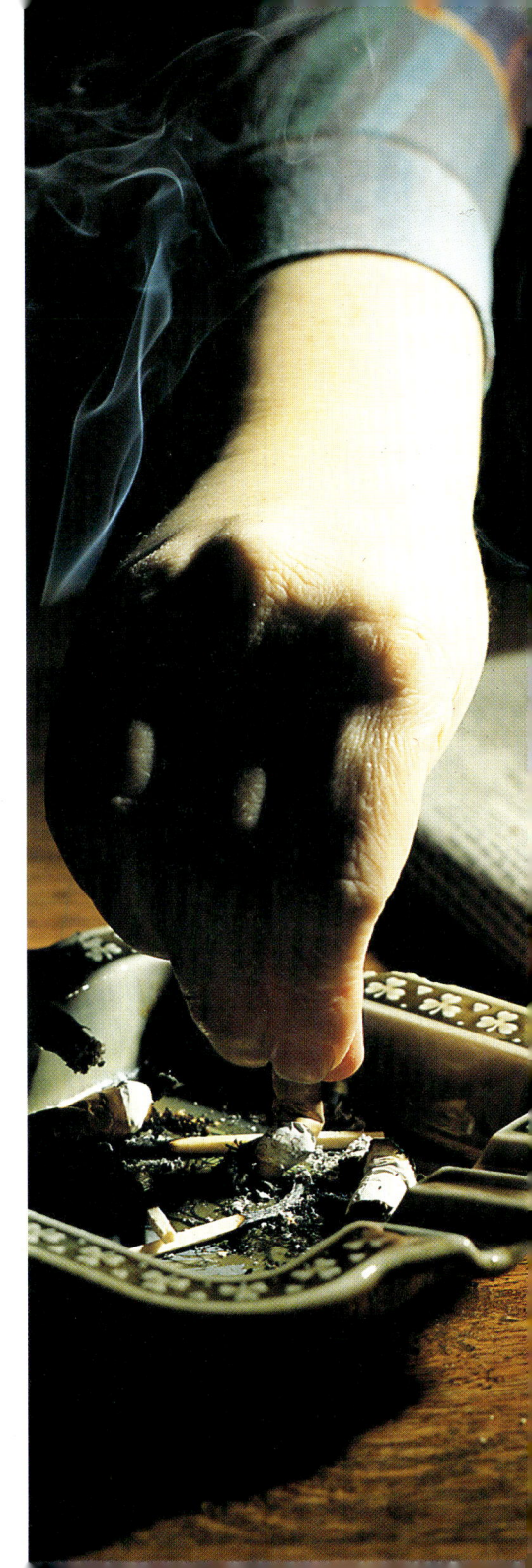

Look after your heart

The United Kingdom has one of the highest levels of heart disease in the world. Heart disease causes nearly one-third of all deaths in the UK in people under the age of 75.

By looking after your heart, you will feel fitter and look better – and you will also be protecting yourself against heart disease.

What is heart disease?

There are many different types of heart disease. The most common and tragic type – the type that causes heart attacks – is called coronary heart disease.

Your heart like any other active muscle in your body, cannot do its work unless it gets enough oxygen. The coronary arteries are the blood vessels that provide your heart with a rich and continuous oxygen supply.

In a healthy person, blood flows easily through the coronary arteries. But these arteries gradually can become 'furred up' with a fatty deposit called atheroma. If the atheroma gets too thick and the arteries get too narrow, the blood supply to the heart muscle can be restricted or even blocked. This is coronary heart disease.

There are two main forms of coronary heart disease: **angina** and **heart attack**.

Angina is the heavy, cramp-like pain in the chest and sometimes the neck, shoulders, and arms that is caused by poor blood supply to the heart muscle. Angina usually occurs after exertion or strong emotion, and is relieved by rest.

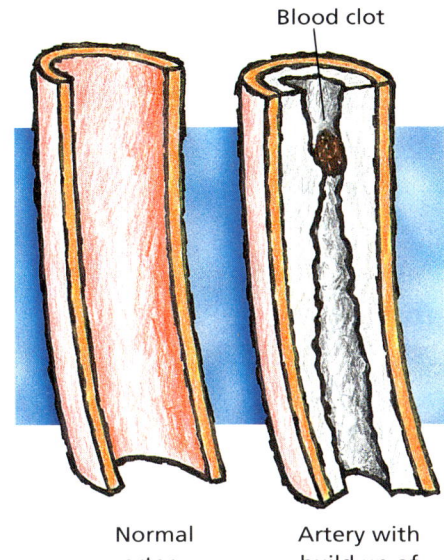

A heart attack happens when a furred-up artery gets blocked up completely, usually by a blood clot, and stops the flow of blood to the heart muscle.

The result is very severe pain, damage to the heart, and sometimes death.

Blood clot

Normal artery

Artery with build up of atheroma

Who gets heart disease?

Research shows that there is no single cause of heart disease. There appear to be several different factors, which together may increase the likelihood of a person getting heart disease. For example, the tendency to die young from heart disease can run in the family; men are more at risk than women; and the older you are, the greater the risk of having a heart attack.

Your age, sex, and family history are all beyond your control, but you can still do a lot to keep your risk of getting heart disease as low as possible.

What can I do?

To reduce your risk of getting heart disease:

- don't smoke;
- eat healthily;
- take regular exercise;
- drink alcohol sensibly;
- avoid stress if you can.

If you follow the suggestions in this booklet you will be well on your way to enjoying a healthier life. **It is never too late to change!**

If you want further information to help you make good choices about your health, then join a local Look After Yourself class (see p. 43).

LOOK AFTER YOUR HEART

Further information

There is a wealth of general health information available from your GP, health centre or local health promotion unit. Your local library should have details of adult education classes on health and lifestyle. You could also look in your local paper to see what's going on in your area.

If you want further information on local health resources and facilities, contact the Health Education Authority, Hamilton House, Mabledon Place, London WC1H 9TX. Tel: 071 383 3833.

The Look After Your Heart: Look After Yourself Project offers a flexible range of healthy living courses throughout organisations and communities in England. For information on how to join one of these courses contact LAYH: LAY Project Centre, Christchurch College, Canterbury, Kent CT1 1QU. Tel: 0227 455564.

Look After Your Heart nationwide

Look After Your Heart is a programme to prevent heart disease and encourage healthier lifestyles promoted by the Health Education Authority and the Department of Health. It is a national 'umbrella' programme under which a wide range of activities flourish. The main areas of work include:

Look After Your Employee

One in nine working days are lost each year due to heart and circulation problems. The Look After Your Heart Workplace Project encourages organisations to look after the health of their employees by introducing a wide range of activities including non-smoking policies, healthy eating, promoting physical activity, health checks and LAYH:LAY classes.

Look After Your Customer

The Heartbeat Award encourages caterers and restaurant owners to take an active role in helping to reduce heart disease by promoting healthy food choices, providing smokefree areas and maintaining good standards of hygiene. Catering establishments meeting defined requirements receive a certificate and the right to display the award and use it in any promotion for one year.

Look After Your Children

The Look After Your Heart Programme is developing a range of national-curriculum-based projects that will promote good health. One example is the Happy Heart Project which will be promoted in primary schools as a key component of the national curriculum.

Look After Your Patient

The Look After Your Heart programme has developed a number of projects that help primary health care teams promote coronary heart disease prevention. These involve general practices in training, materials development and evolving routine good practice procedures in health promotion.

Look After Your Community

The Look After Your Heart Community Projects scheme has funded a wide variety of innovative community projects.

Look After Yourself

The Look After Your Heart: Look After Yourself Project offers a flexible range of healthy living courses throughout organisations and communities in England. There is currently a national network of 2000 tutors.

For booklets on smoking, eating, drinking and exercise write to:
    The Distribution Department,
    Health Education Authority,
    Hamilton House,
    Mabledon Place,
    LONDON WC1H 9TX.
    Tel: 071 383 3833.

For supplementary information on smoking write, enclosing a large SAE to:
    ASH (Action on Smoking and Health),
    109 Gloucester Place,
    LONDON W1H 3HP.
    Tel: 071 935 3519.

For help and guidance on stopping smoking contact your G.P. or local health centre.

There is a national telephone helpline for smokers seeking advice, counselling, and referral to local stop-smoking groups. For support and information, including a Quit Pack ring:
    Smoker's Quit Line
    Tel: 071 487 3000.

For information, publications, and access to a national network of over 40 local councils and advice centres on alcohol:
    Alcohol Concern,
    305 Gray's Inn Road,
    LONDON WC1X 8QF.
    Tel: 071 833 3471.

For general information about a specific sport, ring the Sports Council or the regional office that serves your county:
    The Sports Council,
    16 Upper Woburn Place,
    LONDON WC1H 0QW.
    Tel: 071 388 1277.

For booklets and information on the prevention of coronary heart disease contact:
    The Coronary Prevention Group,
    60 Great Ormond Street,
    LONDON WC1N 3HR.
    Tel: 071 833 3687.

Further reading and viewing

The Health Education Authority publishes a very wide range of resources including leaflets, books, posters and videos. For details contact the address on page 44.

These five publications will help you put into practice the changes we have suggested in this book to help you enjoy a healthier lifestyle.

THINKING ABOUT STOPPING?

Checklist
Do you really want to stop?

Is it worth stopping?
The benefits made clear

Will power
You have more than you think

Where to get help
New booklet explains how to stop. Includes a telephone helpline

---

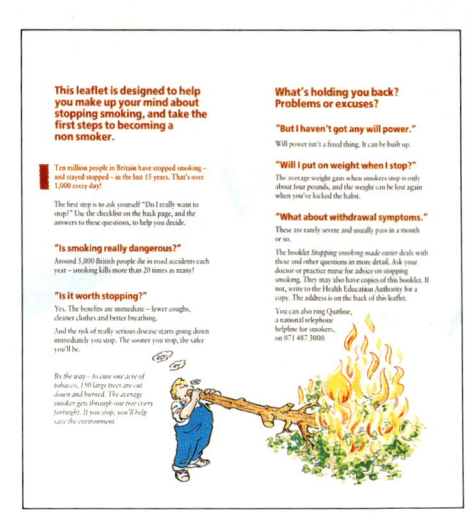

This leaflet is designed to help you make up your mind about stopping smoking, and take the first steps to becoming a non smoker.

Ten million people in Britain have stopped smoking – and stayed stopped – in the last 15 years. That's over 1,000 every day!

The first step is to ask yourself "Do I really want to stop?" Use the checklist on the back page, and the answers to these questions, to help you decide.

"Is smoking really dangerous?"
Around 5,000 British people die in road accidents each year – smoking kills more than 20 times as many!

"Is it worth stopping?"
Yes. The benefits are immediate – fewer coughs, cleaner clothes and better breathing.

And the risk of really serious disease starts going down immediately you stop. The sooner you stop, the safer you'll be.

By the way – to cure one acre of tobacco, 150 large trees are cut down and burned. The average smoker gets through one tree every fortnight. If you stop, you'll help save the environment.

What's holding you back? Problems or excuses?

"But I haven't got any will power."
Will power isn't a fixed thing. It can be built up.

"Will I put on weight when I stop?"
The average weight gain when smokers stop is only about four pounds, and the weight can be lost again when you've kicked the habit.

"What about withdrawal symptoms."
These are rarely severe and usually pass in a month or so.

The booklet *Stopping smoking made easier* deals with these and other questions in more detail. Ask your doctor or practice nurse for advice on stopping smoking. They may also have copies of this booklet. If not, write to the Health Education Authority for a copy. The address is on the back of this leaflet.

You can also ring Quitline, a national telephone helpline for smokers, on 071 487 3000.

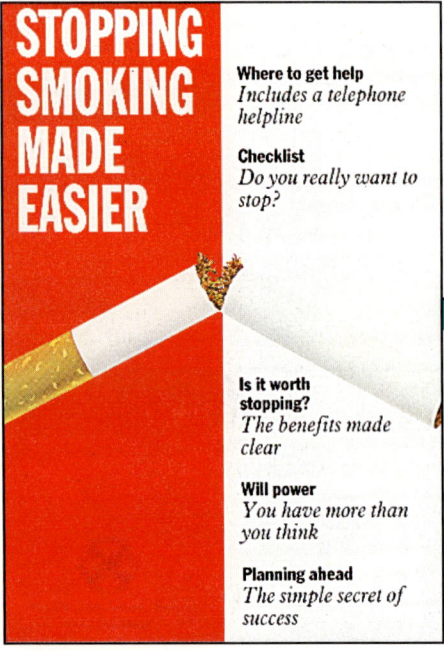

STOPPING SMOKING MADE EASIER

Where to get help
Includes a telephone helpline

Checklist
Do you really want to stop?

Is it worth stopping?
The benefits made clear

Will power
You have more than you think

Planning ahead
The simple secret of success

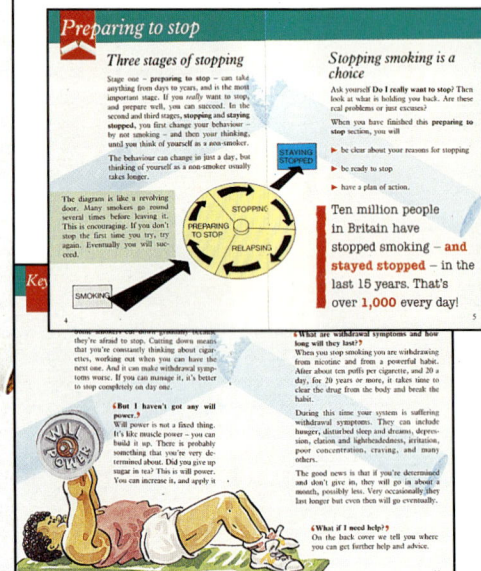

Preparing to stop

Three stages of stopping

Stage one – **preparing to stop** – can take anything from days to years, and is the most important stage. If you really want to stop, and prepare well, you can succeed. In the second and third stages, **stopping** and **staying stopped**, you first change your behaviour – by not smoking – and then your thinking, until you think of yourself as a non-smoker.

The behaviour can change in just a day, but thinking of yourself as a non-smoker usually takes longer.

The diagram is like a revolving door. Many smokers go round several times before leaving it. This is encouraging. If you don't stop the first time you try, try again. Eventually you will succeed.

Stopping smoking is a choice

Ask yourself **Do I really want to stop?** Then look at what is holding you back. Are these real problems or just excuses?

When you have finished this **preparing to stop** section, you will

▶ be clear about your reasons for stopping
▶ be ready to stop
▶ have a plan of action.

Ten million people in Britain have stopped smoking – **and stayed stopped** – in the last 15 years. That's over **1,000** every day!

---

they're afraid to stop. Cutting down means that you're constantly thinking about cigarettes, working out when you can have the next one. And it can make withdrawal symptoms worse. If you can manage it, it's better to stop completely on day one.

6 But I haven't got any will power.9
Will power is not a fixed thing. It's like muscle power – you can build it up. There is probably something that you're very determined about. Did you give up sugar in tea? This is will power. You can increase it, and apply it

6 What are withdrawal symptoms and how long will they last?9
When you stop smoking you are withdrawing from nicotine and from a powerful habit. After about ten puffs per cigarette, and 20 a day, for 20 years or more, it takes time to clear the drug from the body and break the habit.

During this time your system is suffering withdrawal symptoms. They can include hunger, disturbed sleep and dreams, depression, elation and lightheadedness, irritation, poor concentration, craving, and many others.

The good news is that if you're determined and don't give in, they will go in about a month, possibly less. Very occasionally they last longer but even then will go eventually.

6 What if I need help?9
On the back cover we tell you where you can get further help and advice.

47

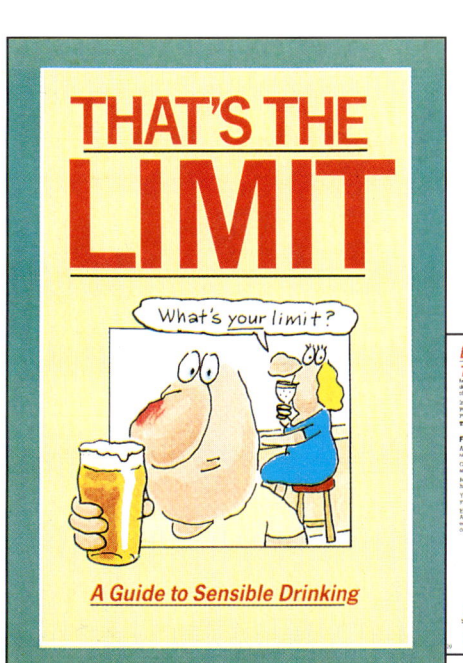

© Health Education Authority 1993.

ISBN 1 85448 479 6.

Health Education Authority,

Hamilton House,

Mabledon Place,

London WC1H 9TX.

Designed by A.R.T. Creative Partnership.

Picture credits:

Hugo Dixon
Page 23.

Sally and Richard Greenhill
Pages 1, 3, 4 (Top Right, Bottom Left and Bottom Right),
26, 27, 29, 31, 34, 35, 38 and 40.

Robert Harding
Pages 2, 22, 30, 32 and 37.

Chris Knaggs
Pages 4 (Top Left) and 9.

James Meyer
Pages 6, 7, 8, 10, 11, 12, 13, 14, 15, 16, 19 and 23 (Bottom).

Photofusion
Page 24.

Printed in England 1000m 3/93